The Ledge

How and Why We Should Boldly
Confront the Struggles of Life

James Bowers Johnson

For Cory, Heather, Timothy, and Emma

May you come to understand how and why both struggle and
suffering are essential to knowing yourself, God, and His will

And not only that, but we glory in tribulations, knowing that tribulation produces perseverance; and perseverance character, and character, hope. Now hope does not disappoint, because the love of God has been poured into our hearts by the Holy Spirit who was given to us.

Romans 5: 3-5

The Holy Bible, New King James Version,
Copyright 1982, Thomas Nelson, Inc.

Note: All definitions at the beginning of all chapters are taken in whole or in part from Merriam-Webster's Dictionary and Thesaurus, 2007.

Dear Warrior,

Without the ability to relate with others, life would be meaningless. Beyond doubt, it is the very act of relating which adds merit to our being. Yet, just how and why are we able to relate? The answer, in part, is by and through experience. When we experience, we come to appreciate situations, conditions, and our sundry states of being. We acquire context as to what others endure. We understand the parameters of life and all it means to be alive. Thus, we relate.

How is this understanding ultimately realized? Through struggle. Struggle brings distinction to experience. Struggle distinguishes opposites and the varying degrees between each. For example, one does not truly understand what it means to be cold if he does not know what it means to be hot. Without knowing both hot and cold, one may not relate with those who experience either or both.

The illustration of a rubber band explains this dynamic. When in a state of rest, the rubber band is not stretched. It is not challenged. It does not experience extremes. The rubber band withstands nothing other than comfort. As such, it will not appreciate a state of rest since this is all it knows. Simply stated, there is no contrast. However, if twisted and stretched, the band will experience tension and, when tested to the extreme, risk being snapped. The band comes to know the distinction between comfort and exertion.

Struggle provides a clear distinction between happiness and sadness, weakness and strength, joy and anguish, ease and effort.

We appreciate the sweetness of victory against the bitterness of defeat. Triumph is glorious to the dread of failure. This is contrast. Contrast by and through struggle is why tribulation is essential to our *being*. With such context, we acquire even greater and deeper experience and, thereby, relate with even greater meaning and purpose.

Shortly before publication of The Ledge, a lady poignantly expressed the value of struggle. She shared a vignette from her past. She was on the Potomac River and grappled with a fear of crossing daunting rapids. The circumstances overwhelmed her. She was scared. This struggle brought a striking contrast to her life. She confronted a choice—remain on the river bank or risk being bold. In the end, she chose to cross.

As she negotiated the forceful rapids—as she persevered—one of the random and defining variables of life happened. She lost her footing and was suddenly swept away by the forceful current. Tossed to and fro by the violent river, she began to cry—not because she was afraid, not for any harm that might befall her, not for failure. No. She cried because she dared to be. She rejoiced because she conquered fear, for being brave at the sacrifice of her safety. She had aspired for what was possible. For this she was grateful.

This lady acquired profound experience when she stepped boldly into one of the many storms of life and endured struggle which offered contrast between comfort and insecurity. With newly acquired understanding, she may relate with those who choose to be safe or courageous. Struggle defined and refined the meaning and purpose in her life.

I was struck with this lady's character and integrity. She was intelligent, articulate, sensitive, honest, inquisitive, self-initiated, strong, caring, independent, resilient, spiritual, and visionary among other attributes. Her potential was incredible. Moreover, she sought to be other than her past. She had struggled for years and now wanted to be all she was able. I was intrigued and wanted to know the extent to which she was ready, willing, and able to relate. For, earlier, I had observed indicators which revealed reluctance and inability. So, I probed until I knew with certainty.

After a dynamic conversation about several topics, the discussion took a notable turn. When she expressed her thoughts and emotions about ongoing legal issues with her ex-husband, her demeanor changed. Her body language, words, and attitude were markedly different. She was the antithesis to whom she had been for the last three hours. The indicators became apparent. She was inhibited by herself and others—all from struggle she had not yet overcome, akin to making a choice to cross a rough river.

While minor struggles are often isolated and have limited impact, larger struggles affect us at a depth and breadth with extensive repercussions. Crossing fierce rapids in a river leaves a narrow imprint while wrestling with divorce is pervasive and profound. While we may successfully contend with minor struggles, we wallow for years with trials that shape our entire being—shaping that is not constructive.

Struggles destroy until they are rightly divided. We prevail when struggles occur with clarity. On the other hand, trials that are riddled with confusion are largely insurmountable. They are not resolved. River rapids may stymie someone unless and until the rapids occur in a way that precipitates growth and a coveted victory. The same is true for weighty divorce challenges. If not discerned, one becomes embittered and angry. When there is no resolution, one is mired in defeat.

This lady shared that she had trust issues and was guarded in relationships. These limitations were pronounced as she expressed her legal woes. If she was to meaningfully and purposefully relate with her own self and others, she had to overcome post-marital struggle as effectively as she conquered the rapids, regardless of the results. If *swept away* with a choice to relinquish meritless legal disputes, she might cry for joy and surrender to a battle she never needed to fight. She might be liberated and enjoy healthy and profound intimacy and be available for relationships in the truest sense of the word.

We all struggle. Everyone fears the ominous unknown. Sometimes we succeed. We also fail. We fail when we perceive struggle in a way that denies victory. When we do not rightly divide inordinate trials—when we fail to discern—we experience defeat. Not surprisingly, humanity relates with defeat more than victory. Our state of being in defeat is distinct from being in triumph. Our *being* and ability to relate are directly affected by how we view struggle. How struggle occurs to us is and should be defining. This is a revolutionary thought.

The Ledge is a story about my son Timothy who, when he was eight years old, persevered through a struggle upon a ledge— The Ledge. One Sunday, he and I reached a ledge above a waterfall with the intent to jump into a boulder-filled pool of water. It was a feat that would unnerve most boys.

As Timothy stood upon this ledge, he anguished simply because of how and why the struggle *occurred* to him. He became and was his own enemy. His very perception of the tribulation *would produce* or it *would not produce*. His perspective would sideline him in defeat or propel him to victory. Would he be timid and fearful or strong and daring? How would he relate with himself or others as a result?

If being and relating are the essence of life, it is essential to understand the experience of struggle. If we discern what it means to be angry, compassionate, scared, joyful, loving, forgiving, or hot and cold, we will *be* and we will *relate* with greater meaning and purpose.

This is especially true for the spiritual. Man seeks to know himself and his divine purpose. Factoring the element of time, the import of relationships, and the need for purpose, man's search for spiritual truth will not be satisfied unless he struggles. Failure to either struggle or rightly divide trials renders life less than fulfilled. It prevents us from knowing ourselves, God, and His will.

Man's *being* concerns life and death. It is between these two tandems that he either survives or thrives. Appropriately, then, we must define the words *tribulation, struggle,* and *suffering.* The Ledge grants each word equal footing while advancing the premise that inconvenience is not struggle. Tribulation, struggle, and suffering shall be defined as the *pressure wrought by experiences that bring forth growth to the soul and spirit.* This definition avoids the slippery slope of relativism. Tribulation is not relative; it is real. Suffering serves a purpose. It enables one to truly live, to *be a life* full of meaning, and allows one to relate. <u>The Ledge</u> explains how and why.

Times of testing are, arguably, the best of times, when we gain through loss. Such is the irony. For example, it is only when we endure hunger that we value having enough to eat. If always satisfied, we would not know what it means to suffer from a lack of food. There would be no contrast. Thus, hardship underlies understanding. We gain when we persevere. Our muscles are stronger when they are exerted. When we struggle, we grow.

The loss of one's leg would be suffering. The same is true with the loss of a parent or child. Is being stuck in rush-hour traffic and lost in an unfamiliar city struggle? I lost a parent and children. Yet, the anguish I endured from being lost in an unknown area almost equaled the death of my father, but in markedly different ways. How could this be? The answer rests with an honest appraisal of all that it means to be human amid the impact of a particular plight. Was I late to a job interview that would shape my entire life? If so, snarled traffic is significant. In the end, it is not a matter of comparing death to lateness, but measuring the impact of each.

Regrettably, most people merely exist and are rarely tried. A mere existence reflects a void of experience and abject ignorance. Then there are those whose lives are desperate; their suffering is second nature. The trials of those who merely exist would be trivial for those who are tested. Is there any doubt that growth from struggle is directly attributed to one's perspective, capacity to endure, and willingness to understand?

Romans 5:3 states that tribulation produces. What does it produce? Perseverance, character, and hope. This is a powerful, spiritual truth. Scripture describes men and women who suffered and persevered with greater character and a sure hope. Jesus suffered. Through suffering, He persevered. Persevering, His character was revealed. With character, He hoped. When we persevere, our character is revealed and we hope.

If we do not appreciate how and why struggle is fundamental for a life of purpose, if we fail to embrace trials, if we live in comfort without weathering storms that would make us stronger and wiser, will we manifest God's intent? Imagine living without ever truly being. Do you want to become who God intended you to be? Do you seek to know yourself, God, and His will? If so, do you discern with the intent to understand and conquer struggle, or are you tribulation's perfect victim?

When Timothy confronted this struggle upon the ledge, how did he think, feel, and act? Did he succeed or fail? Did he value struggle and embrace a world of possibility that would have otherwise remained unknown? Did he appreciate who he was and might become, especially considering divine providence?

As with the lady who braved the river rapids, Timothy was overwhelmed with a fear that affected him profoundly. He had to persevere through a struggle that might reap character and hope. *Tribulation produces.*

Timothy's story ends quite unexpectedly. As you are drawn to his struggle upon the ledge, as you learn how and why he wrestled with adversity, may you appreciate how the challenge occurred to him, a perspective which affected how he related with himself, his father, and life, and, assuredly, with his God.

Each chapter has a listing of four words. These words describe how and why struggle is essential to humanity. The listings represent a progression and, ultimately, a common denominator within man. The first word is either a deficiency or a beginning for the remaining three words. To illustrate, *knowledge* is a beginning from which one will advance into *understanding, wisdom, and truth*. To be *blind* is a deficiency, while *reflection, discernment*, and *possess* improve upon our ability to see.

The last words in each listing, combined with the last words of all listings, support an idyllic spiritual state achieved through struggle.

Truth, Conquer, Obedience, Redeemed, Death, Liberation, Possess, Blessing, Spirit, Clarity, Eternity, Trust, Surrender, Love, and Worship

When confronted with fierce river rapids, the anguish of divorce, or a leap from a ledge into a pool of water, we must persevere. The Ledge is our battle plan—a war manual! We will know victory more than defeat as a result of persevering through tribulation with character and hope. May each of us become conquering warriors!

To your possibility and God's glory,
Your fellow warrior,

James B. Johnson
June 11, 2016

Contents

Foreword

Standing upon a ledge can be scary and a struggle for most of us, especially if we are faced with the choice to jump. The Ledge is a definitive authority that distinguishes the elements of learning, growing, and achieving our best by overcoming struggle.

It has been said, *"Worry is a thin stream of fear trickling through the mind. If encouraged, it cuts a channel into which all other thoughts are drained."* Consider that just a little worry may engulf your whole life. The author, my friend Beau Johnson, takes great care in dissecting the DNA of man's ability or failure to rightly discern struggle as a path to victory. The fear within us need not be. Beau explains how and why struggle may occur for our benefit and God's glory. With his insight, you will appreciate how and why we must leap from any number of ledges and step boldly into the storms of life.

Timothy's story is a deeply moving and greatly inspiring account of how and why "struggle" is a key ingredient to be all God intended. In fact, after reading The Ledge, you will be moved out of your comfort zone and into, as Beau says, a world of possibility.

Consider the "Rule of Threes" taught in survival courses. In survival mode one can last three weeks without food, three days without water, three hours without shelter in extreme conditions, and three minutes without air. But you can't make it three seconds without hope.

Beau reminds us that the constituent parts of HOPE are struggle (suffering), endurance, and character development. These pages offer the reader HOPE! So, whether you think you can or you can't—you are right! More importantly, the examples we set for our children may hinder or help them as they yearn to be. Are you prepared to have your sons and daughters know and understand themselves and their higher purpose in life? If so, read The Ledge and teach them how to struggle.

May this book guide you, as it did me, to strive for and experience the joy of leaping when upon the ledge.

O. Carter

Context

How often have we heard assertions from others that they are following God's will? Who has not heard a friend rationalize a choice in the name of providential prodding when the choice is obviously counter to what God ordains?

A husband, who happens to be a pastor, divorces his wife because God wants it so. A mother moves out of state with her children or files a court action against her husband "because I am looking to God, as He is the only one who knows." If the office of God is leveraged for what He desires not, such justifications are convenient for the moment. Many cavalierly couch the indiscriminate as divine decrees. Conversations are filled with the sentiment that one is congruent with a spiritual mandate. But, is it true?

Does God know? Yes. However, He knows what we know not. We, invariably, do not know God's intent. Such is the state of human nature. We are woefully ignorant of God and His will simply because we are ignorant of ourselves. This is the heart of the matter. At what point do we reconcile this dilemma? When do we cease the self-deception and seek truth?

God reveals truth by means of contrast found in tribulation.

Tribulation severs us from what is comfortable and leads to a dependence upon God and allows us to hope without fabricating indiscriminate desires. Contrast. It is not enough to read or discuss our way into a genuine and intimate relationship and grounded understanding of our Creator. It is through tribulation that we acquire an ability to rightly divide struggle and possess truth. Contrast.

When we become victims of suffering, we understand less. When we adorn our struggles as symbols, if we perfect our role as victims then divorce may lead to cynicism and dejection until truth is obscured. The death of a spouse may spur rage and reclusiveness. The irony is that struggle assures the possibility of persevering as we gain character. Does cynicism or rage reveal character? Does hope flow when the lessons of tribulation are shunned? No. This is contrast of great import. If we fail to comprehend times of testing, if we willingly accept that we are consummate victims, we reject stretching and tearing into knowing and possibility.

I once received a letter from my ex-wife. She disclosed her move to Florida with our children. She said she was *trusting God*. I was not on some military deployment. I was not at the behest of an employer away from home. No. I was incarcerated in a jail with seventy other men. I was waiting to be sentenced for a federal crime I did not commit. I experienced the same conditions as those who sold crack cocaine or committed assaults, grand larceny, and attempted murder. Life as I knew it had ceased, and included not having contact with my children. Treated as a convicted felon was bad enough; not having access to my family was more than I ever imagined. My spirit grieved, especially after I received her letter.

She refused to answer my phone calls. They did not visit. They did not respond to my letters. Complete separation from those I loved was unbearable. How was God using this struggle for my benefit and His glory? What did he want me to learn through perseverance? How was I to respond? Would I avoid revelations of suffering? Would I embrace my circumstances as inconsequential and understand God's will?

When I received that letter, I was sitting on a steel bunk anchored to a concrete floor. With much anticipation, I hoped for choppy handwriting from home-schooled children and pictures, or a belated Valentine's Day card hand-drawn by earnest and loving hearts with a simple "I miss you, Daddy!" There was nothing. My heart sank. I was devastated. I was alone. I was lonely. I was on the brink of brokenness.

With no place to hide raw emotions, I sought refuge. I left my bunk in the middle of "F Pod" for that of another man in the far-right corner. I feigned reading a magazine. The pages appeared as a blur. I avoided eye contact with anyone who walked past. Yet, I could not prevent the inevitable. Tears began to fall and became a stream and then a torrential downpour. Attempts to control my weeping accentuated the heaving of my torso and contractions of my gut. My emotions were deep. The anguish was incredible. The loss was great. I struggled to reconcile our children not having contact with their father for four years. What was God's will?

The stark contrast in life is surprising. The men in F Pod had pictures of their children. They received visits from wives, ex-wives, and children. These men represented the worst of society, predominantly uneducated, poor, abused, abusive, and violent. Some were addicts who faced up to twenty or more years in prison. What did God want me to learn?

I was a college graduate, a former Military Intelligence officer in the United States Army, a white-collar professional who provided for and spent all my time with family. I did not golf on the weekends. I did not have a weekly poker or bowling excursion with the guys. I did not indulge in drugs, cigarettes, or any other vice. Marriage and family were sacred. What did God want me to learn? Whatever His plan, I would not know as a victim upon the ledge with an unwilling attitude or a closed and vindictive heart. Only with utter dependence would I understand that tribulation produces.

Such is the role of contrast. The choice to embrace suffering is not one we would make if only because it is not normal. We choose the opposite. We avoid pain. We reject adversity. We resist. We sit in tribulation like a mallard duck in a torrential rain with feathers impermeable to wetness. We deflect any benefit from the raging storms of life. We refuse to listen. We counter any wisdom with already established positions. We lash out in anger and selfishly re-stake previously asserted claims.

We brood and argue. Such acts are tolerable because acceptance is not. Spite and contempt rule the day. Depraved indifference to humanity becomes a sour creed. Vision is blinded by emotions. We are myopic. Our thoughts and feelings are deep and intractable. Our bodies suffer the detrimental effects of stress. We age. We get sick. We harm ourselves and those lured into and trapped by our plights. Spouses, children, and friends contend with the direct and residual aftermath of senseless battles in an unwinnable war. Our souls are vanquished from the outset as spirits grieve untransformed minds, the hardness of hearts, and defeated wills.

Sadly, we see no alternative to how we handle suffering. Our conditions become a reality. We are comfortable in our misery. This is what we know of ourselves. Such a predisposition is unflattering and certainly not glorifying. We are not teachable. Hope is not possible when we are hopeless. Suicide is an option. Divorce is decided. Alienation is agreeable. Seclusion is sought. Judgment trumps joy. Hate is heightened. Forgiveness is forgotten. We perpetuate unhappiness and we are satisfied. We become vested in a joyless existence. The familiar is manageable. We fuel what we control—we control what is acceptable. We are unable and unwilling to suspend disbelief as to what could be with new possibilities.

This unwillingness renders us quite incapable of change. We live reckless lives fraught with discontent. We do not learn about ourselves. We do not learn about God. We do not learn about His will. We exclude what could be transformative in the most unlikely of places—within suffering. We fail to appreciate that we gain through loss. Contrast.

As I wept uncontrollably, I knew I was without recourse. I did not want to go on. I resigned myself and did not want to endure. I surrendered. I was broken. The circumstances were as they would be. I did not care if I died. While I was not suicidal,

I saw life as incredibly empty and meaningless. It made no sense to persevere when I was unavoidably dependent upon God. Is such a reaction dishonoring? Not wanting to persevere does not preclude enduring. I could not escape the orchestration of God's plans.

Herein rests the beauty of discerning the merits of struggle within brokenness. By God's grace and mercy, I was in despair. I had to choose to accept what was previously unthinkable. I was upon the ledge and could not alter the circumstances. I had to choose *not* to be with my children for years. From this loss, I surrendered to His sovereign will. With nothing to reconcile, there was no need to battle. I trusted in someone much larger than myself. I came to a liberating truth: I could not prevail without my Father. Oneness.

I came to know myself in my weakness and sought refuge in God's strength. With time and discernment, through experience which leads to truth, the harshness of life chips away at the illusion that we are in control. Each successive struggle is God's appointed path to our dependence. When we deviate, we are lost and subjected to loss. We do not gain when we stray, when we follow what misleads. There is no benefit when we run from providence. One is not vulnerable when one is callously indifferent. Ironically, God desires our vulnerability. He wants us displaced, unsettled, and tried. He wants and calls us through tribulation, a sure path to knowing, understanding, wisdom, and truth.

This is my hope for my children. There is no greater goal than to ensure their character through perseverance. Valuable lessons, the greatest lessons of life, can only be had through pressures which bring the weight of unnerving change. Who as a parent does not stress service over self, sacrifice to indulgence, or any noble intent to that which is pedestrian? Do we direct hearts and minds through times of tribulation and shed light upon what is an empty and meaningless and, all too often, purposeless existence? Struggle cuts through the confusion. Contrast.

My life has been one of struggle and sorrowful loss. But for past trials that forged character out of perseverance, I would not have discerned the content of my ex-wife's letter with understanding. Countless leaps from innumerable ledges peppered across my past provided me with perspective. As nature withstands ravaging storms which relentlessly demand submission, the suffering of five decades reduced my soul to a humbling acknowledgment that any contrived agenda was unworthy and maligned paths or perceptions were not sound and would not satisfy or glorify.

But for tribulation, I would not have experienced mental, emotional, and spiritual gain through loss. I would not know myself as I do. I would know God and His will even less. Through suffering, I possess greater truth. Tribulation produces. Contrast. This is my hope and my hope for my children.

Enamel and Enamor

enamel – a glasslike substance used to coat the surface of metal
or pottery; the hard outer layer of a tooth; glossy paint that
forms a hard coat
enamor – to inflame with love

A creator protects his work against loss, deterioration, and ruin. We
preserve objects to maintain their condition. This is a worthy
principle. A fine piece of jewelry is adorned and then protected in a
box. An expensive vase is placed securely upon a mantle. Ornate
and gold-lined china is used for special occasions and then stored in
a cabinet. These items serve a purpose and are enjoyed for their
uniqueness and craftsmanship. They are bequeathed to others in a
near perfect condition. After all, the creator did not create with the
intent to destroy.

When objects are used regularly, they deteriorate. A football is
scratched and scarred and the leather reflects years of play. Any
amount of reconditioning will restore the surface to a degree, but
wear and tear remain evident. The impact of time and lack of use
also have an adverse impact. Prudently, then, the creator takes a final

precaution. He seals his work before stating, "It is good!"

An artist sprays his pastel drawing. A woodworker covers his table with a stain and a coat of lacquer. A sculptor applies glaze to his porcelain which he fires in a kiln. A carpenter primes and paints his house. The creator preserves the fruit of his thoughts, efforts, time, and talent. If only because he values his creation, he guards against damage. The creator is practical and wise.

For the purpose of The Ledge, the act of preserving a finished product shall be referred to as *enameling*. To enamel is to protect something to eliminate the deleterious effects caused by use and time. Enamel, a hard outer layer, shields from harm. Now, let us consider why we would question the relevance of enameling in the first place. The application of a protective layer calls into question having no protection at all.

Suppose an inanimate object became a sentient being. Would there be a need to stain, lacquer, glaze, prime, paint, or enamel it? Would there be a need for protection? The answer may appear transparent and conclude there is a benefit. However, we would be wrong. If an object were alive and enameled throughout the course of its life, would that object not be limited or restricted from experience? If experience is the means to broader and deeper knowledge, understanding, wisdom, and truth, would enamel not diminish any experience from the outset?

Consider an autographed football showcased in a box. If it were never on the field and denied the chance to be in the heat of battle—the defining contest—if it did not endure rigorous testing that would lead to understanding, the football would be what it is, sheltered. It would know nothing other than what it knows. The football would merely exist. Now, is an enameled football that is also on the field of play not the same? Yes. Enamel denies full exposure and prohibits a comprehensive context of being. Enamel is a barrier that inhibits knowing and understanding.

Knowing and understanding what? The answer is not only experience derived from all circumstances, but revelation acquired through struggle. Enamel blocks the footballs of the world from total engagement. What is the purpose of life if footballs do not persevere through experience without enamel? Do they ever really become?

Apply this question to humanity. Are we being? Do we become? This is the heart of the matter. Before answering, we must ask the obvious. Are we enameled? Were we created with a glaze, a covering, a hard layer of protection? No. We are uniquely vulnerable.

What is the relevance of this thought? Why question if we are enameled when we are not? The answer requires a proposition that may not be transparent. While we are not enameled, we are in a precarious position. By our own design, even if unwittingly, we apply a self-imposed impermeable cover which is far more resistant than enamel. We are *enamored*. We become and are enamored with distractions that malign our willingness and ability to be in the truest sense of the word. We are disengaged. We are not being if only because we do not relate.

Man's failure *to be* is a result of distractions. Thus, the use of the word enamor is deliberate. To be enamored means to be captivated with delight or fascination and even a love of something. While this definition does not necessarily appear negative, we must weigh man's intent for engaging that which enamors and measure any subsequent repercussions. With or by what does one become enamored? To delight in or to be fascinated with something, someplace, or even someone in an unhealthy sense has an impact.

Yet a word of caution is warranted. To be enamored, whether knowingly or unknowingly, is not necessarily the equivalent of idolatry. Rather, to be enamored suggests a very subtle or apparent preoccupation of the heart and mind. Enamoring generally is quiet, persistent, and often insidious.

We may be enamored with sports, alcohol, work, food, fitness, television, physical attraction, gossip, politics, money, poker, our own children, hobbies, fashion, and more. Distractions incrementally and continuously block us from being. If we are not being, do we not deny the possibility of experiencing the rigors of life? Insulation and protection within the comfort of what we know deprives us of what we know not. As a result, we foreclose challenges that would otherwise test us. We do not persevere in, with, and through adversity. As a result, we fail to know ourselves, our Creator, or His intent. This is a travesty. Failing to struggle, we fail to *be* in every sense.

When enamored, we are consciously or subconsciously consumed and the repercussions are the same, if not worse, than if we were enameled. Damage from enamoring is far more pernicious. Why? Because we make the choice to be enamored. We become impediments to our being. We deny possibility and are shielded from exposure that is vital for fully understanding what we experience, experience that is essential if we are to relate with ourselves, others, and God.

Consider that every layer of enamel further separates an object from the natural, just as enamoring detaches man from the natural and divine. Enamoring deprives man of experience which would otherwise mold him as his Creator intended. Just as we were not created with a protective cover, we were not created to shelter ourselves within the contrived.

If we realized just how and why enamoring prevents and discourages the possibility of being and the revelation of God's plan, would we not be humbled? If only by our own act of becoming enamored, we remove ourselves from experience. Absent the ability and willingness to spurn the effects of enamoring, we are less vulnerable and persevere less. We have less character and, consequently, we hope less—all from the lack of struggle.

When God finished His creation, He "saw all that he had made, and it was very good."[1] When He created man, He did not apply enamel. We were created without a protective cover. God's creation was finished, but we are not. We have a lifetime to become as He intended. This is by design. To be and to become is not necessarily God's responsibility, but ours. Regrettably, much keeps us from being. Enamoring is one.

Several questions were asked earlier. Is a work worthy of protection? Yes, but we are not complete. Is the Creator wise to keep us safe from harm? Yes. However, God is wise to allow adversity to define and refine us for our benefit and His glory.

Does the Creator handle His creation with care? Yes. But we should not presume our vulnerability is not an element of God's design.

Enamel protects objects from the elements, including time. Enamel ensures longevity. But, not only are we unaware of the length of our tenure on earth, we are exposed to inevitable tribulation. Ironically, we may live longer if we weather challenges and understand the attendant effects as we become stronger and wiser. Our ability to persevere is the raison d'etre, the joie de vie, the beauty and essence of life—that is, if we rightly divide the experience.

Rightly dividing experience and discerning struggle is the essence of being and is acquired from the culmination of knowing, understanding, and wisdom. This observation brings us back to a core premise. *We will not know ourselves until we struggle.* Consider a rather obvious query. If man were enameled, would he persevere less than if not protected at all? If we are not made with a protective cover, why would we choose to be and remain *enamored?*

The Value of Tribulation

When the soul is untested, preoccupied, or far removed from the spirit, we fail to know God and His will. Moreover, if we do not know how or do not care to discern struggle in our lives, we less aware of both the soul and spirit. Conversely, if ready, willing, and able to appreciate how and why suffering is essential for growth, we would reap the blessings of tribulation. With discernment we would understand spiritual truth. Truth is attained with knowledge, understanding, and wisdom, all of which are acquired from and through adversity. Truth and suffering complement each other by their interconnectedness. Through suffering we may possess a greater understanding of truth.

Since we were created in God's image and reflect His nature, should we not be perfected in this light? Surrendering to this goal is a worthy endeavor which would require us to depend upon Him. What is the path to dependence? Tribulation. Tribulation strips away the pretense and lies—trappings which often obscure truth. Tribulation purges the heart and mind of deception that blinds. Tribulation allows us to answer the queries: Who am I? Who is God? What is His will?

Isn't our response to God crucial? While God is sovereign and all is sourced in Him, is He not the progenitor of our faith? Do we not have a response to His sovereignty? Do we not have a choice to be and become as designed? Do we not have a choice to acquire greater understanding through struggle?

God seeks our response. He wants to relate with us. Moreover, He is glorified when we faithfully obey. A more congruent relationship with God would be that much more glorifying. Yes, to God be the glory as we come to know Him and His will through tribulation. Since our response is integral to knowing God, how we respond to suffering is of equal import. Suffering is a means of extrapolating life to the divine and a point of departure from what is *unknown* to what is *known*. Absent struggle and discernment, we are denied this knowing.

Romans 5: 3-5 reflects a scriptural truth that underscores the value of knowing through tribulation.

And not only that, but we glory in tribulations, knowing that tribulation produces perseverance; and perseverance character, and character, hope. Now hope does not disappoint, because the love of God has been poured into our hearts by the Holy Spirit who was given to us.[2]

Man does not typically glory in tribulation. To glory during times of testing is counter to human nature. Notably then, if we do not glory, do we ultimately *know*? What is it that we fail to know? The answer is found within the rightly divided and discerned context of perseverance, character, hope, tribulation, and love. For, mere suffering is not enough to know God. Knowing that tribulation produces is vital. The word *produces* connotes that tribulation must be discerned. Otherwise, suffering is for naught.

One may languish through trials with an attitude of rebellion and never gain what could be. A lack of discernment is not profitable. Divorce is a tribulation. If one suffers the loss of a spouse and family and remains an embittered and vanquished victim, the fruit from such tribulation is unknown. Loss through divorce is difficult. However, knowing tribulation is worthy of glory avails character and hope through perseverance. The value of knowing through tribulation is underscored by asking: What do we gain when life is placid? The answer is relatively nothing. God intended that we suffer and that we come to *know* as a result.

Since God encourages suffering, He calls us to persevere with understanding. This is as an act of love. Consider the life of Jesus. He was upon the ledge, if you will. He suffered to redeem a sinful people. Through His death God was glorified. Jesus sought and accomplished his Father's will. This was His calling. He lost all so that God would be all. Jesus was denied so that God would be glorified. By His example, *knowing that tribulation produces perseverance, character, and hope* has never been more aptly illustrated.

Jesus, the Christ, came to know Himself, His Father, and His Father's will by suffering unto death. Jesus suffered and became wholly dependent upon God. He had no inhibitions, false fronts, avoidance schemes, or pretense. He did not escape into the unreal. He was not enamored. He was broken and this state allowed Him to *be* completely vulnerable and malleable to His Father's will. He was faithful and obedient through suffering. Tribulation produces.

Fatherhood

Father. Little did I know how ill-prepared I was for this self-appointed role. Honestly, are men ever prepared for this humbling responsibility? While some are more predisposed than others, the art of fatherhood may rest in one's willingness and ability to assess and adapt with the hope to be and become the paternal example God intended for a child's benefit and God's glory.

Fathers have a mandate to affirm their sons and daughters. A father's affirmation of his children is fundamental to their very being. This one act is instrumental if fathers are to shepherd children throughout life. Declaring a child's worth is the greatest gift a father can offer. This act of love has a direct impact on how a child relates to himself and others and affects how he contends with experiences and struggle.

As I reflect upon my childhood, as I weigh my father's influence, I know why I would accept or reject his example. Given the enormity of my influence as a father, the affirmation of my sons and daughters was critical. I sought to reinforce their strengths and improve upon weaknesses so they would be strong, confident, and self-sufficient. How was this to be accomplished? I did not necessarily know. But my desire was unquestionable.

I developed a philosophy that when children understand their relationship to experience and struggle, their perspective broadens. When they comprehend how and why their souls affect them, they intuit that experience and struggle have a purpose that should not to be shunned, but embraced. Children deserve to struggle. If they are to be men and women of character who are obedient and faithful, they must understand that adversity is a natural component of life. When they understand tribulation, children may more effectively govern their minds, hearts, and wills—their souls.

The mind, while the very source of man's creative nature, is often his nemesis and riddled with doubts that bind and manipulate. "You can't do that!" "You don't have the guts!" "What will people think?" The heart is equally crippling. Emotions blind. Anger, jealousy, love, frustration, and hate often deceive us to the exclusion of understanding. Finally, a man's will can be rather formidable, especially when influenced by the mind and heart. One may defy a providential appointment without the least consideration. A man with the intent to follow a given path regardless of the repercussions is a will unto himself and not to be dissuaded. Ultimately, one may govern his soul with understanding or remain in confusion.

He who learns to master his soul by and with discernment is pruned by struggle. He is, often without awareness, shaped by adversity. Given that the soul does and must serve a purpose, the benefits of adversity are vital. For example, if a man's home were on fire, his mind would likely focus with problem-solving creativity; his emotions would enhance his ability to perform; his will would compel him to act with power. Or, if a man climbs a 1,000-foot cliff without ropes, using nothing but powder and his God-given strength and talents, his mind would have a singular intent. His emotions would be grounded. His will would be resolute. His life would depend upon deliberate discernment and effort.

Our willingness to know God's will is essential. God created us with a spirit, soul, and physical body. The alignment of all three is paramount if we are to live providentially. Noteworthy, although God is sovereign, we have a responsibility. He calls us to be engaged. He wants our participation. He invites our sacrifice. He expects our obedience. He longs for our faith. He wants our dependency. If we are to know God and His will, we must know who we are. The suggestion that we simply wait and depend upon God is wanting. We have a divine decree to be actively and willingly vulnerable and our discernment of tribulation is essential to this end.

If we seek a fulfilling life, not just an ideal existence, acquiring an appreciation for the context of struggle is critical. Struggle satisfies a role. God wants us to contend. He wants us to battle and to know and understand more after persevering. Tribulation produces.

Consider the plight of humanity. The fall of empires reflects the demise of the once strong. Such observations instruct on a macro scale lessons that may be applied to the micro—to man. Rome fell. This once mighty empire collapsed for several reasons. At the heart was a lack of will to be as it was formerly. The people lacked the strength and resolve to persevere with character into hope. Thoroughly enamored, Rome lost its soul to obsessions and became unmoored within its decadence. This world power slowly succumbed to a decay that crippled its people who were no longer willing to struggle.

The founding of America and the enormity of the Puritan's passage from England are notable. Consider the inconceivable odds pilgrims faced upon the seas and when they landed. They struggled. They confronted peril, disease, starvation, and threats which brought out their best. They were not distracted by the artificial. They were not enamored. They withstood all and were compelled to rely upon God's craftsmanship of their very beings.

The settlers who moved out west and staked land claims were no different. Their journey and challenges were inordinate. They traveled by wagon into hostile territory. They braved the elements and contended with adversity and death. With limited provisions, they built homes of sod without floors and windows. They planted crops and had limited livestock. They endured harsh winters and burned twisted grass for heat. They depended upon themselves and each other as communities survived and thrived through grit and faith.

Compare and contrast their lives with ours. As they persevered through tribulations which revealed their character, did they not come to know their God and His will? Did they not have a greater dependence upon Him? Were they not deceived less? Were they not more directed to a congruent spiritual end?

Countless have weathered struggle to a revelation of their true selves—the true beings God created. Reference to *beings God created* is deliberate. By and through tribulation we may be. This is axiomatic.

We need only examine the growth of a plant to understand why adversity is fundamental to being. A seed is not alive until it is planted and watered. Then the miracle of tribulation unfolds. With warmth and moisture, the seed changes. The plant struggles to emerge. The seedling strives to break through its outer membrane and anchor roots for stability. It perseveres as it breaches the surface of the soil. Exposed to the light of day, the fight for survival begins. It weathers the heat, cold, wind, rain, and predators. Whatever the challenge, it grows to be as God designed.

Our lives are no different. Why would we avoid the struggles of life? Why would we avoid being? Even when a flower is in full bloom, manifesting its beauty and purpose—*being*—it still endures. When it reaches full potential, the struggle toward death is no less. Living a finite number of days, the petals wither and eventually fall. Humbled by age, the plant weakens and droops. Having survived and thrived in life, fulfilling God's plan and purpose in the bounty and necessity of struggle, the flower surrenders to death.

Is there any doubt that God wants the same for and from us? He does not want us protected. He does not want us enamored. He does not want us to wither before our time or fail to become who we could and should be. He wants us to struggle, to anchor roots, and to strenuously breach into possibility. He wants us to battle with greater knowing and understanding.

God created us to persevere into character and hope, to be alive, to be a life manifested for His perfect end. The path to this hope is not through apathy, abundance, distractions, or mindless engagements. This hope is not realized by existing in what is confused and contrived. This hope is borne out of trials. Our challenge is to struggle and *be* valiantly in all circumstances.

Raising children as if they were prized possessions is the antithesis of our charge as fathers. Protecting children from struggle denies them a world of possibility and lessons which benefit their bodies, nourish their souls, and move their spirits. Consequently, when fathers do not relate with their sons and daughters about the virtue of struggle, when fathers do not help their children discern the benefit of persevering, then fathers prevent them from relating with themselves, others, and life. Simply stated, if fathers inhibit struggle, they fail to affirm their children's worth as warriors

My perspective as a father directly affects how I relate with my sons and daughters. When I am with them physically, I drop to their level for eye contact. Yet, I share intellectually and emotionally in a manner that draws them to language and ideas beyond their age and experience. I relate with them in a manner that prepares them for the rigors of life.

For example, we do not have television. I dispensed with this insanity the day I left my parent's home. I read with my children and tell them grand stories. I engage their minds. Whether at home or away, we converse, name, explain, spell, and question anything and everything. We did not baby proof our home, which typically reflects an attitude anchored in fear. My children are free to touch and explore. The refrain of "No!"—the alarming and accepted mantra for raising children—the rallying cry of the ignorant and condemning, which defeats young minds and spirits, is not what they hear.

If they attempt to do something, anything, they do so to the extent of their capabilities. Obviously, they will not do what is beyond their means. However, if they are inclined to attempt what they believe is possible, I encourage and assist them. With my watchful eye, they experience life to the fullest without a an overt injection of reservations and fear.

My approach may be an aberration and my children certainly do not enjoy some aspects. For example, they are not allowed to have video games, which reduce life to a linear and mindless existence. We were created to relate. Children flourish when they engage others and life. Involvement with family and friends is essential. Our countless hours of wiffle ball and kick ball far exceed a meritless sedentary existence. They explore physically, mentally, emotionally, intellectually, and spiritually. They succeed and fail. They thrive in both victory and defeat. Anything to the contrary is not being.

My perspective often clashed with the views of others—those with attitudes which reflected impossibility. For example, Timothy's decision and actions once collided with a negative and controlling perspective. When he was young, he was on the front porch with relatives. He then came inside and asked me a question. I noticed his changed demeanor. He was subdued. He wanted to know if he could play with a simple hand tool, a three-prong rake for digging in the flower garden.

Given his altered disposition, it was apparent something was awry. I responded to his tentativeness with unwavering encouragement. "Absolutely!" He had used this tool previously. It was no more threatening than other toys or objects he handled and he did not play with this tool with an attitude of fear.

I followed him as he returned to the porch. I watched as he haltingly secured the rake and looked cautiously at those present. He expected to confront the same attitude he encountered moments earlier. He said rather softly, "My Daddy said I could play with this." He had been told he could not do what he knew was possible.

A negative influence is destructive. I was sobered by the impact on my son. I was humbled and grateful that he lived in a positive and encouraging home. He was not subjected to control and condemnation; rather, he knew optimism and possibility. My children lived with the freedom to do and be. Success and failure were an experience away. They were encouraged to crawl, walk, run, and fall and to do it again. They were free to test the limitations of their abilities.

They answered a question I asked reassuringly, a query which bound a father and his children. "What do I always tell you?" I asked. "Trust Daddy!" was their confident reply. If they were scared, they would "Trust Daddy!" They were emboldened from their varied experiences and unquestionable paternal support. They knew I wanted them to experience life and relate with me.

When my children fell and scraped their knees and elbows, when they came with tears, I was counterintuitive. Not drawn to their momentary misery, I admired their bravery and admired their new *badges of honor*. I noted their daring resolve with praise, hugs, and kisses. They grew with a positive outlook. Inevitably, after sharing their injuries and woes, they returned to their activities with a fresh perspective. They embraced their father's attitude. It was not uncommon for them to proudly show their "badges of honor" to others. By contrast, reactions of alarm and sympathy limited their experience and sorely affected how they negotiated life's twists and turns.

When we live less reservedly, especially during times of struggle, we acquire greater insight. It is more fulfilling to embrace suffering than to withdraw timidly. The former fosters perseverance, character, and hope, the latter, inhibition and fear. If we know ourselves and our strengths and weaknesses, if we accept loss equal to gain and strife equal to contentment, we will struggle and do so with glorious distinction.

The Ledge
Part One

"Jump, Timothy! Jump!" I yelled. "You can do it!" Balanced among the rocks that lined the bottom of a natural pool of water, which ten seconds earlier cascaded over a waterfall ten feet before me, I gazed at my son. My fingers and feet were white, numbed by the frigid water. "Wahoo, Timothy! You are the man!" I shouted over the thunderous pounding. High above, Timothy stood as if frozen in time. He summoned the courage to step off in defiance of his fears.

Knowledge, Understanding, Wisdom, Truth

Knowledge – something learned and kept in the mind
Understanding – to grasp the meaning of; comprehend
Wisdom – good sense; judgment
Truth – the real body of evidence or facts

Whether by observing, doing, or reading, there are many avenues to knowledge. Knowledge is the foundation upon which we attain truth. Truth is gained by a progression of sorts. First, we must know and then with knowledge, we understand. Understanding leads to wisdom and truth. While not an ironclad equation, it became a father's guide.

Given the importance of their formative years, I steered my children directly into the heart of experience. They saw, thought, touched, and acted. They engaged anything and everything. They were immersed in life which meant they were not sheltered from life. I encouraged them to be and do. Their heads, hearts, and hineys were involved. They were encouraged to ask questions and seek answers.

Once, in the winter, when Timothy was three years old, he

asked about the creation of ice. I immediately clothed him and drove to a frozen pond five miles across town. The ice was thick enough to bear our weight. We walked onto the frozen water. We touched the cold, smooth surface. We examined the air pockets trapped within the ice. We observed the concentric rings that ran along the shore, evidence of advancing ice from successive days of freezing temperatures.

We shivered as we searched for rocks. If we were able to kick them loose from the frozen ground, we slammed them into the surface of the ice. We learned that the ice with air pockets cracked easily. The clear ice, so clear that it appeared as if there were no ice at all, was thick and impenetrable and the rocks bounced upon impact and slid effortlessly across the pond.

When we were so cold that we did not want to bend our knees, not wanting frozen pants to touch our legs, we stepped back mechanically like robots to the car. We laughed as we sought refuge in the warmth. Once thawed, we braved the cold again. We threw rocks across the ice in the same manner as we skipped them across the pond in the summer. We gauged our success by distance. Then we ran slowly, picked up speed, and slid ourselves as far as we could. We stomped on the air pockets and examined the fragments of ice chips. We noted the thickness, shapes, and angles. We took pieces as souvenirs to show his mother.

This is what we did when Timothy asked about ice. He queried and came to know and understand by experience. Will he remember this event? Unlikely. Will he recall the particulars about the ice? Probably not. But he will build upon this attitude of exploration time and again. He will come to know and understand by experience and add meaning and purpose to his being. With this attitude, he will acquire greater wisdom and truth.

The ice illustration reflects a perspective about life. As my children were exposed to the wonders of their world, they were challenged in multiple ways. When we explored the ice, I explained the concept of weight distribution as it pertained to its thickness. We discussed how the thickness correlated to the expanse and depth of the water. I shared that the ice in the center of the pond was not thick enough to bear our weight, while the ice near the shore would. Timothy heard what was far beyond his capacity to fully appreciate.

I pushed for his expanded emotional wisdom as well. If afraid, we held hands. He would "Trust Daddy!" as we forged ahead. Rarely did he acquiesce to his fears. My children pressed beyond their reservations and embraced each lesson with greater daring. They would *grasp the meaning* and *comprehend* with every experience. Whatever the subject, we investigated. We tested. We pushed. We endured. As they experienced more broadly and deeply with their thoughts, feelings, and actions, they would become wiser.

Who has not met wise men and women? Who does not hope to emulate them? Who does not want wisdom and to raise wise children? The word *wisdom* invokes images of white-haired gurus sitting atop Mount Attainment with eyes as deep as their insight and a calmness which underscores the depth and breadth of their experience.

Noteworthy, the wise do not fall to the top of the mountain. They inch their way up, touching, feeling, and being into knowledge and understanding. When they fail, when a crisis knocks them down, they collect themselves, grab their walking staffs, and dismiss the circumstances. They ascend with broader insight for the failure. Tapping deeper into their souls, the wise assess, test, and prove. They acknowledge their strengths and marginalize their shortcomings. They experience with the intent to know themselves and truth.

Each trial chisels away the innocence and ignorance associated with inexperience, just as a stream carves a crevice through rock. The wise peer not only within themselves, but within the natural and spiritual. They aspire to commune with the Great Spirit, God Himself. Not satisfied with the incomplete, they abide until they are sentient, until they reconcile doubt and gain wisdom.

The wise discard the needless weight of greed and exercise the gentle spirit of benevolence. They shun judgment for the blessing of forgiveness. They reject the notion of hate for the timeless premise of love. They long for the unknown and divine. They express a humble gratitude for the journey. For those who are wise, wisdom is collected and cultivated throughout a lifetime of experience and perfected with a simple equation:

Knowledge + Understanding + Wisdom = Truth.

We fail to apply this formula in a culture which discourages the unorthodox. Probing beyond the convenient and ordinary is considered unnecessary. We knowingly and unknowingly cater to the status quo. We readily accept what is rather linear and shallow. We are uninitiated. We rarely challenge what is *known*. Thus, acceptance of supposed *truth* without any testing falls short of the equation that knowing begets understanding which begets wisdom, a process which may involve loss or sacrifice, the price of admission that is often necessary to acquire truth.

Timothy deserves truth. Every step up the mountain—every struggle—will bring him closer to truth, that is, if he rightly divides tribulation. A life lived in the valley or on the plateau with negligible testing and minimal engagement will not lead him to truth.

As Timothy made his way to the ledge, he began to know and understand just as one assesses a foe. With future tribulation, perhaps a divorce in twenty years or a death in thirty, his leap from this ledge would be one of many trials and certainly minor in comparison.

If he suffers a divorce, will he capitulate and lack forgiveness? Will he be saddled with guilt, judgment, and hate? Will he covet to the point that he does harm? Will he ignore the lessons from the first half of his life to shelter the balance of his life while he destroys the lives of others? Will he stoop to sordid and base instincts which contradict long standing virtues and principles? Will he be pessimistic? Will he feast upon the contemptible and confused? Will he fail to be a man of character because he does not persevere and rightly discern suffering?

Or will Timothy withstand the storm? Will he know himself, his God, and God's will as a result of being in the thick of gut-wrenching adversity? Will Timothy acknowledge life as circumstantial? Will he realize this earth is not his home and his life is not his own? Will he seek the calling of a providential purpose to the exclusion of the conventional? Will wisdom acquired from leaps from life's sundry ledges lead him to hope and truth?

The truth is everything. Confronted with this reducible end, nothing else matters. If Timothy braves imminent death, will he persevere into unmatched wisdom that truth is indispensable? The leap off the ledge is not about the leap; it is about truth.

Consider that:

- Acquired knowledge expands one's capacity to relate.
- Understanding is a bridge to wisdom.
- Wisdom is acquired when struggle is rightly discerned.
- Truth is indispensable. Knowledge + Understanding + Wisdom = Truth is a matchless formula to a life of purpose and distinction.

The Ledge
Part Two

With his arms wrapped around his chest, Timothy shivered. His knees were bent. His feet were immovable. His eyes were fixed upon the water below. He heard me, but he was not listening. He was trapped within the circumstances before and around him. His mind was plying its trade of deceit and doubt. Timothy's emotions were conflicting. His will balked at the challenge. My precious son, in the throes of life, confronted the possibility of being. Would he jump? How would the experience end? What would he come to understand? The wonder of it all.

Unbelief, Trial, Risk, Conquer

Unbelief – the withholding or absence of belief; doubt
Trial – the action or process of trying or putting to the proof;
    test
Risk – exposure to possible loss or injury; danger
Conquer – to get the better of; overcome

Timothy did not believe he would jump. His unbelief was an impediment that prohibited him from risking and conquering. Since he did not have much prior experience, persevering, even to the point of failure, was critical. Otherwise, unbelief would become a common staple, a crutch, a past reference to which he would defer when pressed to perform.

Akin to an unwanted fiend, unbelief becomes contemptible by familiarity. It resides within our souls and gives rise to suggestions of "can't" and "won't" and perpetuates insufficiency and inadequacy. This regrettable posture fosters a sense of inferiority. A cautious boy wrapped in disbelief will become a timid man wrapped in an unbelief that is seasoned and cured for decades.

I often witnessed my children express unbelief, which I countered with optimism and encouragement. I would instill

35

confidence in Timothy. I served as the catalyst that would move Timothy beyond an unbelief that would be resolved with and through this trial. Tribulation produces. If Timothy had submitted to his unbelief rather easily, there would have been little risk and little to conquer. Had he walked to the ledge and did an about-face, had he waved the white flag of surrender, or recoiled within the queasy quarters of doubt, there would have been no tribulation. Conquering is not possible without a contest. Risk must be part of the equation.

Even if battles end in defeat, they should be fought valiantly. Times of trial are pivotal if warriors are to conquer. Picture Timothy upon the ledge as he twisted and turned inwardly. This condition began the moment he made his way tentatively down the bed of the creek to the precipice of the waterfall. Like the water that cycled violently in the turbulence below him, Timothy's angst churned doubt after doubt. He ruminated over what he now considered impossible. His perception became his reality. This is what he knew. Yet, if he persevered, Timothy would know far more than he ever thought possible. Whether he realized it or not, this trial would be instructive. For, wisdom inheres from experience, woven trial by trial into an appointed tapestry of our lives, the details of which God alone foresees. One detail which remained elusive was whether Timothy would risk.

Risk is the consideration which affords a man the possibility to issue a declaration of the will, like a trade or barter, a simple transaction, where the reward exceeds the sacrifice. Did Timothy perceive a reward which merited the risk? The experience upon the ledge was no different than when he learned to ride a bicycle and risked falling in order to gain the reward of speed. While unnerving, the willingness to risk is the point of no return. Choosing to risk is the line of embarkation. Crossing that line leads to conquering.

Consider that:

- Unbelief is a belief that something is not possible.
- To be victorious, beliefs must be anchored in a perspective of resolve.
- Trials are necessary for growth. They provide the experience and confidence that we are able.
- Risk is an act of the will.
- Warriors conquer only when they risk.

The Ledge
Part Three

Two months prior to Timothy's arrival upon the ledge, he and his sister, Emma, hiked with me over a mile up a mountain that is home to a little-known reservoir which sits on a plateau. It is a serene setting, picturesque. The water is warm and still, green, and clear. At the water's edge, a few flat rocks serve as steps which mark the drop-off into the depths. Minnows and small fish dart about in search of food.

Pronounced above all aspects of this secluded paradise is the quietness. To shout seems unnatural, as if forbidden. We had the place to ourselves and our laughter and banter were surreal. Timothy and Emma, who reveled in their curiosity and excitement, were the lone contrast to an otherwise tranquil atmosphere. This was our playground for the day and we made the most of it.

In the left center of the reservoir is a large concrete platform rising twelve feet out of the water. Beginning underneath the surface of the water are rectangular-shaped steel rungs anchored in the side of the structure ascending every eighteen inches. This ladder is the invitation to one of the many battlegrounds in a child's life. The moment my children saw the platform, the only artificial element of the setting, they wanted to jump from the top. So, with floats around their arms, we dived into the small lake and swam some distance to the colossal, tan structure. We climbed the rough rungs to the top and were rewarded with the warmth of sun-baked cement under our tender feet.

Not surprisingly, Timothy's and Emma's perspectives were drastically altered. Their vantage from above the water was strikingly different than the one below. I watched their faces. I sensed their astonishment and trepidation. I noticed their subtle and not so subtle reservations. I wondered if they would change their minds. The endeavor was daring for any young child to ponder, to do what a father would not rightly expect.

Except for the sound of the surplus spilling into the drains at the base of the tower, the water was as calm as it was near the shore. The stillness put Timothy and Emma at ease. We were blanketed in peace. The sky was blue and cloudless. The wind was ever so gentle. There were no rocks visible. If any existed, they were hidden at least thirty feet down.

Would Timothy and Emma jump? They had no pressure to perform and no influence to keep them from doing so. They had no pressure to perform and no influence to keep them from doing so. They were with their father, their biggest fan. They knew I would not push them to do what they did not desire. I was there to encourage, regardless of their decision.

Surprisingly, within moments, and to my delight, they did the unexpected. They dropped from the top of the platform and splashed into the expanding depths of who they were to become.

I was as proud of them as I was ecstatic.

Character, Fear, Faith, Obedience

Character – moral excellence
Fear – profound reverence
Faith – complete trust
Obedience – the act of obeying

Life is a miracle. A thin black seed planted in moist soil emerges as marvelous marigolds. Mind-boggling. A flat whitish seed, the size of a thumbnail, grows into a gigantic pumpkin. Amazing. A sperm penetrates an unsuspecting egg and becomes a boy who hopes to leap from a ledge. A blessing.

The physical appearance of a child reveals only a smattering of the story. Beyond his features are his soul and spirit. His life has yet to unfold. For better or for worse, a father's impact is undeniable. The character we exhibit, the pressure we apply, the lessons we impart, and the thoughts we express affect our children profoundly. Will they be moral and obedient? Will they be weak or strong? Will they follow and lead effectively? Will they honor their principles? Will they love? Will they forgive? Will they push beyond what is comfortable and sacrifice for a worthy cause? Will they become wise? Will they honor their word? Questions abound. A father is critical for the answers.

When an author writes a screenplay, he develops the plot. He choreographs the scene and directs the protagonist to the left or right, into danger or back to safety. This was my role with Timothy upon the ledge. I provided directions, dialogue, and dramatic tension. Would I ridicule the main character as he stood upon the ledge? Would I call him a "Sissy" and laugh with derision? Would I break his spirit and prevent him from daring? Or would I acknowledge him as a champion whose life depicts the plight of the human spirit? Would he summon the courage to venture where the timid shudder to go? When a father scripts a child's life, there are consequences.

I want Timothy to be challenged. I want him to struggle and persevere into character and hope. I want his muscles to strain, his lungs to heave, his heart to race, his mind to turn, and his will to anguish.

Timothy's character will be the continuous thread of his being. If he lacks adversity, his character will be revealed even less. If he experiences true suffering which epitomizes the deepest gut-wrenching loss, he will possess character into unexpected blessings. Any struggle which breaks him will be for his gain. This may be a foreign concept to a coddled culture; yet, Timothy's journey through times of desperation should be more rewarding and valued than his enjoyment of peace and tranquility. Undoubtedly, failure to equip him for the unknown assures his demise.

We honor and respect those who prevail during times of great difficulty with extraordinary effort. We revere them. Reverence, often defined as fear, reflects how one views life. A man who reveres both his father and God bestows honor and shows humility. In this context, fear is positive.

Will Timothy dignify his body, soul, and spirit with the fear and wonder they deserve? As he perseveres into greater suffering, his understanding of fear will deepen and his faith will broaden, especially as he submits more obediently. Obedience is a telling measurement of reverence. A father is honored when he is obeyed. Often, I did not honor my father in this respect. I was afraid of him. His use of force was alarming and riveted my attention. I complied with his commands simply because I was scared.

I saw this attitude as an officer in the Army. Soldiers respected one's rank regardless of the person. Yet, a superior who was not worthy of his position or authority, be it for abuse, pride, or a lack of ethics, was not feared. He was not one to whom deference and honor were granted. I willingly obeyed a commander worthy of honor and often performed beyond his expectations, fulfilling not just his legal orders, but the spirit of each. However, a commander who was not worthy of respect had obedience absent reverence.

Experience, especially through suffering, provides context and affords us an appreciation for those who deserve respect. Will Timothy revere himself, his father, and his God? If not, does an absence of fear denote a lack of testing? Will he obey with a desire to honor and not out of mere obligation or intimidation? If so, why? The reason may be that he lacks the knowledge and fear of himself, all from the absence of suffering.

There is a correlation between obedience and perseverance. Timothy may endure a trial, but if he does so in disobedience or with a dishonoring spirit, he may not reap what his father and God want him to gain. If one is obedient without fear, does he lack the hope of what may be confidently embraced and does this equate to an absence of faith? Struggle will reveal a man's character and his reverent dependence and obedience would be an expression of his faith.

Faith, it may be argued, is the adhesive that binds fear to obedience and obedience to hope. As men faithfully persevere, their reverence deepens into obedience and hope. Timothy hoped the day he was upon the ledge. He hoped to reap what was sown in his relationship with me, namely, honor, love, and trust. The unknown was whether he would sacrifice. If he did sacrifice, he would do so with faithful reverence.

Timothy's struggle upon the ledge could be inspiring. If the audience saw a boy who revered his father, they would see a leap of faith from a son who feared a man he hoped to emulate—a hope that originated with a struggle. They would see a boy who feared himself and possessed a hope of what was possible.

Such perseverance would be glorifying to God for several reasons. First, tribulation produces and we become as God intends. Pressure brings us closer to God's manifest intent. Second, God takes quiet satisfaction when we overcome trials. We share in His shaping of our lives as we willingly shoulder the burdens of life. Finally, God is a conquering God. He battles mightily. Are we to do any less? God delights in the camaraderie of willing warriors, those intrepid spirits who persevere and honor His divine will.

Consider that:

- Character is wrought by adversity.
- Fear is reverence for whom and what are worthy.
- Faith binds fear to obedience and obedience to hope.
- Obedience is a barometer of the humble and noble.

The Ledge
Part Four

Now upon the ledge above the waterfall, Timothy faced an experience quite dissimilar from the concrete platform at the reservoir and certainly not as high. He confronted an unexpected challenge of his mind, heart, and will. He would be tested and, whether he prevailed or not, obtain a clearer understanding of himself in the face of adversity. Moreover, even if he did not realize it, in some small measure, he would gain a greater understanding of God and God's will for his life.

As Timothy stood upon the ledge, as I encouraged him, I was struck with the enormity of the scene and pressures upon him. While all struggles are similar in many respects, each has a separate context nonetheless. I am certain God relished the contest of boy against himself as much as I did. This was true the day Emma and Timothy jumped from the platform at the reservoir.

Undoubtedly observers are directly affected by those in the heat of battle. Their observations are defining and add meaning to their lives. Emma was now on the sidelines. Yet, she certainly had an appreciation for Timothy's dilemma. The drop she made at the reservoir was one of the gutsiest and most inspiring. I will never forget how she inched her toes to the edge and then stood motionless. Quite like an Olympic platform diver, she acted only when she knew she was ready. She was as bold as any six-year-old and her form was perfect.

Although Emma made the choice not to jump from the ledge, she vicariously understood her brother's challenge. Additionally, out of love for Timothy, she was vested in his daring effort. She would be influenced not only by the tribulation, but she would be moved by Timothy's performance. The impact may be greater for those on the periphery simply because they generally are unable to affect the outcome. They are beholden to what is.

Vulnerability, Mercy, Grace, Redeem

Vulnerability – open to attack, susceptible to wounds
Mercy – compassion
Grace – an act of kindness, courtesy, or clemency
Redeem – to ransom, free, or rescue

In a conversation with a friend, I remarked that life was delicate. She disagreed. She said life was strong. She was correct. Life has an enduring quality which reflects vitality and strength. But life is also vulnerable. Both attributes are complementary. Strength is borne from vulnerability just as vulnerability requires strength. Out of loss, we yearn to be.

Nature's resiliency is incredible. Carnage in the wake of a hurricane exposes how assailable life is. Desperate conditions demonstrate how plants, animals, and humanity are at the mercy of fate. Though tested and humbled, nature perseveres and its character is revealed. Nature prevails time and again as it burgeons back to its original state. When we contend with the formidable, we suffer, often quite miserably; yet, with strength, we endure.

A husband and father may be blindsided by a divorce. The

abject upheaval from his wife hiding their children in the home of another man is raw destruction. He is vulnerable, but he perseveres. He heals and hopefully understands himself through such loss. Others, however, suffer the same tribulation and become calloused and indifferent. They glean little insight. They are not vulnerable; they do not endure. Such retreats deny strength. Whether by death, divorce, discord, or dearth, determination and daring are critical as a matter of course.

Timothy was vulnerable upon the ledge, which was as it should have been. When I was a young boy, I strived to do more than I was able. I feigned my true self. This posture offered me a false sense of protection. At times I was not vulnerable. Everyone hides. We create false fronts. We become inflexible and are not teachable simply because we are not exposed.

If Timothy honestly and unabashedly assessed himself in and through suffering, he would be vulnerable and, as a result, become stronger. Regardless of the circumstances, if he possessed what he was able to understand, Timothy would grow. He would discern what was important and embrace principles and values gained predominantly through loss. In his vulnerable state, by persevering, he would be wrought into a man of character.

It is by virtue of mercy, which denotes empathy and compassion, that I entreat Timothy's struggle in life. Through mercy, Timothy endures trials for his betterment. Anything to the contrary would not be love. He cannot and will not avoid struggle. As with nature, he must prevail. Ironically, mercy requires that he endure times of testing. I empathized with

Timothy as he struggled upon the ledge. I did not want to quiet the storm or quell his emotions and supplant the courage requisite for victory. Timothy alone had to persevere into what he needed and wanted. He had to contend with what afflicted his soul.

My objectives were sourced in compassion. I did not shield Timothy from hardship. If I followed our cultural inclination to pave the path of comfort for Timothy, I would have denied him the attendant strength he would gain from his vulnerable nature.

The emergence of a butterfly from its cocoon demonstrates this principle. As a butterfly grows, it struggles to free itself. When successful, the butterfly can lift its wings and fly. If we assisted and opened the cocoon prematurely, if we made its debut struggle-free, the butterfly would perish. Mercy requires that the butterfly struggle. Is there any doubt mercy required Timothy to be vulnerable into subsequent strength upon the ledge?

As the pressures of life bore down upon Timothy, as he withstood the onslaught, his character would deepen and his understanding would expand. He would survive and thrive. Unbridled suffering is indispensable. This is mercy. Since God is love and He seeks to do good and not harm, He provides the mercy we need to endure.

I never intend to harm Timothy. I seek his well-being. I am his father; he is my son. Through this relationship, he trusts me. I hope for what is best for him. If it were possible to usher him directly into the unfathomable glory of God, I would do so only by encouraging him to surrender by and through suffering.

Through his vulnerability and subsequent strength, acquired with perseverance that produces character and hope, he would meaningfully enter the orbit of God's will. Timothy's character is the substance that will allow him to know with a hope that God is sufficient.

The sufficiency of God is best appreciated by knowing we were redeemed by Christ's suffering. God provided grace to redeem the unredeemable. We must mirror this posture as we shepherd children through abject need. Grace is essential. Degrees of kindness and clemency are critical for warriors who are burdened in the heat of battle, especially an unwinnable contest.

We were created for God's glory. Since life is a battle, showing up for the confrontation is defining. Is it not obvious that all else is circumstantial? In the grand scheme, nothing else matters. This representation provides an appropriate parallel with Timothy's struggle upon the ledge.

The redemption he sought from the natural circumstances he experienced upon the ledge would be gained through sacrifice. As such, Timothy had no cause to be unreasonably demanding; for he lacked understanding. He had to be merciful to himself; for he lacked understanding. As his father, I had to provide mercy and grace; for, he lacked understanding. Any failure to attain redemption would be from efforts sourced in ignorance and void of mercy and grace. The more Timothy exerted himself without understanding, the more difficult the struggle became. His effort would be spent in vain. This was his practical reality.

Once resigned to his vulnerable state, once he granted himself mercy, once grace was extended, Timothy would reach the beginning of understanding and the point of surrender. His effort was not required. Surrender would provide him with resolve. At this juncture, Timothy could simply walk into the heart of the struggle as opposed to fighting.

There is a direct correlation between understanding and vulnerability and strength. Timothy would acquire understanding simply because he was vulnerable into strength. His vulnerability precipitated and his strength validated redemption. In the end, all circumstances would be rendered meaningless and his surrender would be defining.

Consider that:

- To the wise, vulnerability is strength.
- The strong are merciful and allow themselves and others to fail.
- We must grant grace to warriors who enter the fray.
- By God's example, we must redeem others whenever possible.

The Ledge
Part Five

We traveled to the country to reach this secluded spot. The majestic Shenandoah River is just a stone's throw away. Along a quiet road among the towering sycamores, elms, oaks, and maples, some of which had been there for centuries, a creek catapulted off a ledge and raced to the river. Access to the creek required a steep descent of a thirty-foot trail. To misstep would be to fall. For support, we grabbed vines, branches, and roots lining the path to the water's edge.

The creek was filled with huge rocks and mighty boulders. The noise from the waterfall was deafening. The cliff to the right and dense vegetation to the left trapped the sound. Its only escape was to rise into the moist air or flow with the mist and water downstream. Fifteen feet before us was a pool of water some twelve feet deep. The pool was pounded into submission by the crushing volume of water charging over the ninety-degree drop. The sheer force drove the cool mist directly into our faces. Any remaining water from above flowed discreetly along an embankment to the right and nearly hidden by low vegetation.

Conception, Birth, Life, Death

Conceive – to form an idea; imagine
Birth – rise, beginning, or derivation from a source
Life – the period from birth to death
Death – the end of life; the cause of loss of life

Life is comprised of cycles. Cycles are everywhere. The sun rises.
The sun sets. The tides roll in and recede. Geese migrate.
Seasons change. Storms conquer. Mating rituals persist. From
beginning to ending, cycles provide a rhyme and reason for all
we experience.

Some of the cycles in our lives are obvious; others are subtle.
Within our bodies and souls, we experience the ebb and flow of
life. Cycles are woven, moment by moment, with seamless
orchestration into even greater cycles. Even if cycles are more
abrupt from accidents or death, we continue towards either
harmony or disharmony. We acquire balance and perspective
with and through the randomness and permanence of cycles. We
survive, thrive, live, and die through cycles.

We conceive. We devise and design which gives substance to
ideas. Conception is the wonder of creation. Who has not

inspired to create or created only to be inspired? God is a creative Being. He conceives and creates. We were created to conceive. As we plod or race through life, we often take for granted the power of conception and corresponding cycles and sub-cycles.

Conception gives birth to what is not. Thought begets thought which begets possibility, a new beginning within the grand cycle of life, a never-ending cycle. A new thought adds meaning to what already exists. Life blossoms and flourishes with a purpose until death. Death, the termination of the conceived, is the end of a cycle and no less part of life's congruent and perpetual nature.

When we stopped to view the captivating waterfall, we declared, "Let's walk down to the bottom!" Conception. The thought was spoken into existence. Birth. We trekked to the base of the trail where the water surged. Life. When we arrived at the creek's edge, the idea and act were accomplished. Death. Our minds, the creative engine of our beings, conceived a new idea. "Let's swim in the water." Birth, life, and death. Within cycles, life continued harmoniously, just as the sun rises and the moon bows in deference. Ceaseless cycles.

The significance of cyclical influences within human nature is defining. Cycles illuminate and educate. They inspire and discourage. How we relate to cycles is telling. My effectiveness as a father is directly attributed to my sensitivity and insight gained from cycles. There is undoubtedly a cycle to my being, just as there is a harmonious cycle with how I relate with my sons and daughters. I cherish this dynamic.

Sometimes my influence must be one of disharmony. Disharmony is consistent with conception, birth, life, and death. Consider the following: "Let's jump off the ledge!" Conception. "Yeah! Awesome idea!" Timothy and I climbed the path we had descended moments earlier. Birth. Life unfolded as father and son attempted to do what moments before did not even exist. The challenge upon the ledge was a sub-cycle, within other cycles, within the greater cycle of life. This sub-cycle involved a minor struggle. Struggles are but cycles contained within macro cycles that are disharmonious until resolved. The leap from the ledge was a conception of doubt, birth of confusion, life of stress, and death by defeat, surrender, or victory.

Timothy had climbed the trail with a sense of daring. But after we entered the creek and walked toward the ledge, his enthusiasm waned; his steps slowed; his zeal died suddenly as he approached and then stood upon the ledge and confronted the terrifying prospect of leaping. Cycles within cycles.

Meanwhile, I climbed to the top of a tree trunk which had fallen and landed across the creek and directly above the ledge, rising a few feet above the moss-covered rocks. Cycle. As my son looked on, I leapt with a boldness illustrating the ease of this feat. Cycles interacting with other cycles. I yelled, "Geronimo!" as I plunged into the pool of water. Death. An entire sub-cycle was executed within seconds.

When I surfaced, I secured my feet amongst the submerged rocks. I locked my eyes on Timothy and encouraged him. "Jump, Timothy! Jump!" Conception, birth, life, death. Cycles everywhere, within everything. Timothy was not hopeful. The struggle overwhelmed him and blocked what was possible—a leap conceived minutes earlier. Cycles which countered cycles, provided contrast, contrast sourced in struggle which revealed the richness and fullness of life.

While it would have been inspiring if Timothy had jumped off the ledge without hesitation, the challenge would not have been as great. Struggles occur when cycles counter existing cycles. Conflicts ensue when two opposing forces confront each other. Timothy's conflict depicted hope grinding against hopelessness. Such a battle would shape him.

Tribulation produces perseverance. Perseverance produces character. Character produces hope. Cycles. Conception, birth, life, death. Cycles have been and will be woven into Timothy's life. As he wrestled with circumstances upon the ledge, which were circumstances beyond his control, he had the possibility to be larger than who he had been previously. Life. Yet, potential failure, no less a cycle, waited forebodingly. Life.

As I encouraged my son, I took great satisfaction in the fight. I conceived and gave birth to words and strategies that would influence how the situation occurred to Timothy. Cycles engaging cycles. Who would he be as a result of his experience? What would he understand? What would be revealed? What would perseverance produce? Would he hope any more or any differently? Questions reflect the bounty of cycles and their importance. Timothy had to ask and answer questions.

Ironically, Timothy, in the thick of this experience, would face death. This is the contrast which makes life worthwhile. This contrast is the oft misunderstood or never understood nature of our being. Death within cycles, especially disharmony from struggle, exposes our weaknesses and underscores our strengths. Death severs the pretense of the mind and heart—the contrived, feigned, and false fronts. How? By the rawness and realness of cycles. Conception, birth, life, death.

Whether from inexperience, pride, ignorance, or lies, we are forced to confront the unexpected, the travails that expose our inadequacies and incompleteness. We realize or are reminded that we are not as we once perceived. We are humbled and this is yet another cycle. Cycles never end. Blessed is the man who embraces the possibility of death throughout the cycles of life.

The essence of death is distilled by contrast. If Timothy lacked disharmony and death within an empty and meaningless life—a life void of purpose—he would exist within cycles which offered nothing. There would be no challenge. Like asking Timothy to dig footings three feet deep so we could build a deck, struggling with hard labor, something he would reject, what would he gain? Anything and everything. Death.

Digging would require that he contend with adversity. He would be tested as he learned of muscles he never knew existed. Death. As he endured the contempt for such unwanted physical exertion, his heart would pump, his lungs would expand, his thoughts, and emotions would react harshly. Death. His patience would be tried with rocks entrenched in thick, moist dirt. Death. Each struggle originating from the act of digging would give birth to anguish that would battle his preferred pleasures. Death.

Whether he realized it or not, Timothy would inevitably *die*.

He would acquire the understanding that, with death, his old self—his prior way of being—passed away and he became anew. Cycles. Cycles within cycles. Cycles countering cycles. Cycles engaging cycles. Cycles creating cycles. Harmony and disharmony. Conception, birth, life, death.

The death Timothy faced upon the ledge was greater than an easily negotiated leap. Had he jumped without hesitation, I would have applauded his confidence; however, he would not have been tried and tested. There would have been no bending, twisting, severing, molding, or straining—no arduous battle of the mind and heart. No vise would have pressed his will to decree for the difficult over what was not.

Admittedly, some cycles are better than others. Some cycles, often the road less traveled, afford the possibility of rejecting the old and accepting the new and, invariably, the unknown. Recall the caterpillar which becomes a butterfly, wholly dependent upon struggle out of the cocoon for its survival. Death into renewal. Within the ubiquitous cycles of nature, the context of struggle is revealed when sharply contrasted with what is normal. The disharmony of struggle, which must be acknowledged as quite harmonious within the cycle of life, adds purpose to an otherwise indistinct existence.

God wants all of us. He wants all of me. He wants my son. He wants us dependent. How does this occur? Dependence does not occur during periods of comfort. Tranquility does not give rise to the insurmountable. Abundance of what is good and pleasing does not strip a man to a humble understanding that he is desperate. Man has no need to persevere when satisfied.

Character is not a by-product of what is facile. Who hopes when there is no reason to hope?

Given the inherent value of tribulation, there are cycles which breed what is uninspired and should be avoided. The cycle of complacency is one. There are concepts which should not be dignified and concepts which should be prized far more than they are. Our gain rests within cycles of disharmony and death. These cycles bring forth growth.

Scripture tells us that "to live is Christ and to die is gain."[3] Gain is acquired through suffering. Each tribulation, each death, is a revelation of truth. Cycles. Disharmony. A leap off the ledge is death and gain. A plunge into an imposing pool of water lined with mighty boulders is a spiritual birth. Cycles. Timothy hesitated. He was not prepared to die. He saw no gain. He lacked dependence. He was without discerned truth. He was at a critical juncture. Like the caterpillar, though, he could persevere through death and emerge as a new creation.

Timothy's hesitation was a good and telling posture. His weaknesses and inhibitions were exposed. His facade was revealed as a fraud. Cycles. Disharmony. He could depend upon his father to provide what otherwise would not have been. His character would be revealed with the providential provisions of a father, ledge, tribulation, and his willingness to persevere. If Timothy chose to endure, he would enter a world of possibility—one of character and hope. Cycles.

As I weighed my son's situation, I willingly availed myself for his benefit. There was no doubt I would assure his redemption in this time of tribulation. Cycles. I loved him enough to have him anguish and die into victory. Cycles. I would sacrifice with him. Cycles. His plight was mine. This was life and death conceived and manifested out of struggle. Cycles.

Consider that:

- We should behold the miracle of conception.
- We should behold the miracle of birth.
- We should behold the miracle of life.
- We should behold the miracle of death.
- Cycles give rhyme and reason to our being.
- Cycles of disharmony ensure growth.

The Ledge
Part Six

At the center of the ledge was a tree trunk that had fallen and now crossed the creek at a forty-five-degree angle. The trunk rose until it was three feet directly above the ledge. It was as if it had been providentially placed for fathers to make their leaps, which is what I had done.

Directly to the left of the tree trunk, on top of the ledge itself, moss covered rocks were ceremoniously laid for those brave enough to trek across the slippery creek bed. This was the appointed place for those brazen enough to stand in the center of this venue. From this spot, the observer, especially an eight-year-old boy, could be overwhelmed with the confluence of such striking sensations. Vividly accented in the water, rocks and boulders appeared as if they were mere inches from the surface and one could kneel and touch them.

Bondage, Imprisonment, Transformation, Liberation

Bondage – a state of being bound, servitude
Imprisonment – the state of being imprisoned; captivity
Transformation – an act, process or instance of transforming;
    conversion
Liberation – free from bondage or restraint; unbind

No one wants to be in bondage to anyone or any condition. I am acutely sensitive to the subtle or obvious chains that bind me. I attribute this sensitivity to experiences throughout my childhood. I also have a brother who is a year older and was nearly twice my size. If I weighed ninety pounds, he was one hundred and sixty. I was small. He was large. I was weak. He was strong. This disparity was reflected in the thrashings he delivered, which were at times intolerable. I grew from these trials. The act I loathed most was being bound underneath him. I detested the pressure and being trapped. I became enraged when he constrained my arms and legs. I despised being held captive and rendered motionless.

    I recall one rare occasion, with my right arm free while

pinned on my stomach, I managed to thrust my fist under the left side of my throat and punch his face. Momentarily loosed by the shock of the blow, I scurried away knowing of the pummeling that would follow.

Naturally, I am sensitive to the undue influence *authorities* exercise over others, which is especially true concerning my children. I recoil when others unnecessarily and arbitrarily impose their will over them. I weighed the concept of bondage as Timothy stood upon the ledge. Bondage, as if by unappointed proxy, denied him the possibility to be bold.

Timothy was imprisoned by his perception of his circumstances. If he could create wiggle room and thrust the proverbial blow that would allow him to act, he would be liberated. Every sight, sound, and sensation, a bar to the cage that locked down upon its metal seat, made him a prisoner. The thundering of the waterfall, "Clank!" The rocks directly below, "Clank!" The cliff to the left, "Clank!" The cold water, "Clank!" The peaceful scene behind him, "Clank!" His doubts, "Clank!" Each trapped him interminably, "Clank! Clank! Clank!" There was but one way out of bondage— the key. The key would transform Timothy and liberate his soul.

If Timothy were to conquer his thoughts and emotions and, consequently, allow for an escape, the circumstances had to occur differently to him. His perception of himself and the situation had to change. This was the key. If the tribulation occurred differently, he would willfully decree an alternative courageous course of action. Altering how the situation occurred was essential for him to cross the divide from unbelief into possibility. I was his de facto accomplice. I would help in his escape.

Timothy's fear brought permanence to his plight and he wrongly divided this struggle. Had he discerned appropriately, he would not have been predisposed to bondage. Although the key to victory was within his capacity, he was not seeking freedom. Thus, I led Timothy to a *knowing* that would reap what tribulation produces. He had to correctly assess the context of this trial and acquire character that would allow him to hope. For he and he alone could prevail.

The telling aspect of his transformation and self-release is that Timothy would never again be deterred by this struggle. His path would be clear once he conquered the tribulation. He would see possibility, not defeat. I had no doubt liberation would lead him to a new occurrence. He would know and be into a physical, mental, emotional, and spiritual understanding beyond what once imprisoned him. This insight would not necessarily be immediate, although it could be; and each successive struggle he endured, however great or small, would add to his collective insight.

Yet, if Timothy deferred to how the situation presently occurred to him and chose to jump another day, he would prevail still. Why? He would have a greater sense of himself. It requires courage to choose—resolve—not to act. To confront a challenge is to be, as Theodore Roosevelt declared,

> the man who is actually in the arena whose face is marred by dust and sweat and blood; who strives valiantly; who errs, who comes short again and again,

because there is no effort without error and shortcoming; but who does actually strive to do the deeds; who knows great enthusiasms, the great devotions; who spends himself in a worthy cause; who at the best knows in the end the triumph of high achievement, and who at the worst, if he fails, at least fails while daring greatly, so that his place shall never be with those cold and timid souls who neither know victory nor defeat.[4]

If Timothy deferred to a healthy respect of caution, he could rightly divide the tribulation nonetheless and account for his strengths and weaknesses. Liberation is not a casual event. It should not be. Liberation demands a dogged resolve, which is why perseverance begets character.

The moment Timothy paused upon the ledge, he was shackled by limitations. His body language disclosed his trepidation. "Timothy stood as if frozen in time and summoned the courage to step off in defiance of his fears." Contrast this image with him inserting the key. The struggle would be a part of his past. Akin to a tumbler within a lock, in which the pins must be aligned to a particular position in order to unseat the bolt, Timothy had to align his will with and through the circumstances he faced. The key—the occurrence which properly positioned each circumstance—would dissipate the discord inhibiting possibility.

Consider that:

- Bondage to truth is alone worthy; any other bondage is only good to the extent we persevere into character and hope.
- When held captive, we must seek the key for escape— how the situation should and could occur.
- When struggle occurs to us as beneficial, we may be transformed into new creations.
- The parallel between liberation and truth is unquestionable. We are freed as we transcend toward truth.

The Ledge
Part Seven

These were the circumstances the day Timothy stood centerstage upon the ledge as he marshaled the gumption to leap. Against this scenic backdrop, fronting this grand but confined and chaotic theater, poised above the imposing below, with the cacophony of bass drums bellowing from the well of the waterfall, as the forest swallowed the creek not fifty feet beyond, Timothy struggled with it all. The atmosphere was loud and violent compared to the tranquillity of the reservoir. There was no doubt my son was now tested in ways he was not upon the concrete platform.

Blinded, Reflection, Discernment, Possess

Blinded – lacking or grossly deficient in ability to see

Reflection – ponder; meditate

Discernment – the ability to grasp and comprehend what is
    obscure

Possess – to have as an attribute, knowledge or skill

Timothy did what most boys would have done. He reacted
impulsively with the intent to execute what he had not fully
considered. He knew his father would leap from the ledge. He
would too. There was no doubt in his mind; at least this is what
he thought. However, once he reached the appointed spot, he
was blinded. As he stood upon the ledge, much was hidden from
him. This often happens in life. Daily we rise to the known and,
at any moment, confront the unknown. When we do, we lose
sight of the familiar. When dynamics change, we are forced to
reconcile the inconsistent from normal or preconceived patterns.

    When Timothy was younger, we went to the store. This trip
started with the obvious. We gathered what was needed. We
walked to the car and climbed into our seats. Everything was

routine until Timothy and Emma saw a wasp flying in the back of the vehicle. What happened? They became manically aware of the unusual. Their thoughts and emotions changed. The wasp radically altered their state of being. They were overwhelmed. They screamed and cried. They recoiled and dodged. They sought protection. They were oblivious to all else. They were not about to consider a different perspective. There is a distinction between the ordinary and the unexpected. Struggle.

Upon the ledge, Timothy confronted something vastly different. A typical trip to the country became exceptional. As with the wasp, he was not objective. He was equally flummoxed. He shouldered self-inflicted pressure and neglected his sense of awareness and powers of observation. This is what we do. We blind ourselves from what is commonplace. The same is true when we grapple with the unexpected. We contend with tunnel vision. Opacity blocks a comprehensive and credible representation of the truth. Timothy "stood as if frozen in time." Recall that "he heard me; but he wasn't listening." Meanwhile, I explained that the drop was shorter than the one at the reservoir. He did not heed transparent distinctions.

Timothy's reflections were not balanced. Like his momentary obsession with the wasp, fearful of being stung, Timothy reconsidered his current situation. Would the water sting? Would he hit the rocks? Was it worth the risk? These were some of the negative thoughts running through his mind. Doubt prevented him from reflecting reasonably.

Timothy had innocently crossed the creek with the intent to conquer the unknown with his father. Once he reached the ledge, his perspective changed. When the wasp was in the car, I encouraged my children to remain calm. In a futile attempt to direct the intruder from their vicinity, I asked them to open their windows and accept the idea that the wasp would not attack. I encouraged Timothy at the waterfall. He had to move beyond what obscured possibility. If he reflected, he would understand differently. He would reckon the truth amidst his extreme thoughts and feelings. He had to discern if he wanted to possess the truth.

The ability to discern and possess truth requires strength and insight that is counterintuitive. We must do the opposite of our natural inclination. When children see a wasp in the car, they become tense. They do not relax. Yet, the latter is the better course of action. Relaxing allows for objective observation. We may then calmly and wisely open the windows and release the wasp—problem solved. Reflection, discernment, possession.

If we weigh Timothy's history as it relates to water, we learn that his experience with the familiar is not what impeded him. Most recently he jumped off the tower at the reservoir. Every summer he used the diving board at Mr. Sullivan's pool. He went down the water slide at the park. He took swimming lessons when he was younger. Even earlier, he grabbed my hands as a toddler and jumped off the side of the pool into my arms— not the water. He had a collective historical context which gave him an *understanding* about his abilities. Moreover, he had the means to draw from his experience.

His history contradicted his current perception. There was a reason why. Something equal to the wasp—the unusual— affected what was seemingly ordinary. If he relied upon what he knew, to the exclusion of the extraordinary, if he calmly walked straight into the battle with confidence, much like rolling down the window to free a wasp, he would discern and possess.

There is a natural progression from blindness, reflection, and discernment to possession. This sequence is elementary when one engages the cycles of struggle. One may not possess when he is blind. One may not discern absent reflection. Who will possess when he cannot see?

Consider that:

- When the obvious is hidden, we cannot see the significance of the immediate or long term.
- Reflection is an antidote to rash reactions.
- Discernment is vital for perseverance into wisdom.
- Possession of truth is possible and should be our priority.

The Ledge
Part Eight

"Timothy!" I yelled over the constant clapping of the waterfall. "This jump is four feet less than the reservoir." Though he acknowledged my observation, he was unaffected. He was transfixed by the torrent and turmoil of his emotions and thoughts. He was affected by any number of factors: the noise, sights, the rocks, mist, the expanse that surrounded the pool, the cliff to the left, and the cold water. Even the peaceful backdrop added to the dramatic tension. To make matters worse, he, unlike the time at the concrete tower, had an audience. Timothy's aunt Holly and cousin Maddie were watching. Pressure powered down upon a boy who wanted to perform.

Lack, Want, Need, Blessing

Lack – to be deficient in
Want – to desire earnestly; wish
Need – to have cause or occasion for, require
Blessing – to give glory to; praise, glorify; to confer happiness
   upon

Who has not considered his purpose as a father? Who has not
weighed a child's lack, want, need, and blessing? Perhaps those
who do not question beyond what they *know*. Given the
significance of raising a child, it is worth noting that we are not
taught the how and why of parenting. We fall in love. We have
children. We largely do what our parents did—wing it. We draw
unknowingly from a perspective based upon unfounded
precedent.

   This approach is problematic. Our children become unwitting
pawns subject to generations of ignorance and incompetence. We
perpetuate the inferior and parent without proper context. How
often has an abused child become an abusive parent? How often
has a child of an addict become a user? How often has a child of the
wealthy become petulant and expectant? Parents must understand

the repercussions of deficiencies, desires, necessities, and the appropriation of bounty.

Consider the following example. A mother slept with her first child from the day he was born until he was two years of age. The mother slept with him in the morning, afternoon, evening, and night. The child became unduly dependent upon her. Not surprisingly, the mother was dependent upon him. The son satisfied a latent void in her life dating to her childhood. As a result, they were inseparable.

The repercussions from this attachment disorder became more severe with time. The son pacified himself as he held his mother's hair throughout the day. He ran his fingers through it with a pulling motion, eventually holding her hair tightly with one hand while he sucked his other thumb. This, too, was also a constant practice. During waking and sleeping hours, the mother compromised her role. She became an object. She was a tool, and the primary force behind the formation of her child's identity. She immersed herself into her son. The mother sowed her sense of insecurity into her child's present and future. Sadly, she allowed her son to do the same with her.

This mother may not have initially known this behavior was harmful; but, when apprised of this concern, she summarily dismissed it. When she became pregnant again, this unhealthy dynamic had to be reconciled. Not only was her husband not able to sleep in their bed for years, the pending demands of a second child would be unbearable. This practice had to cease. Their son had to be weaned from his mother; she had to be pried from him.

The process of separating the two was painful. Over a span of at least three months, the father staged a detox campaign. He purposely lay with his son at bedtime in the child's room. The father then moved to the floor as he held his son's hand who remained in bed. He then sat in a chair directly beside the bed, again, holding his son's hand. The father moved the chair to the end of the bed and eventually to the door. At each phase, the son questioned his father as to why he moved, why he was not closer, and was no longer holding his hand. The father responded with compassion, resolve, reason, and reassurance. Invariably, the son fell asleep hours later and often distraught.

Since parents do not reconcile the lack, want, need, and blessings for their children, the significance of the above illustration is profound. This mother's *parenting* was sourced in her past. She relied upon only what she *knew* and what she wanted. Moreover, what she *knew* and wanted was largely attributed to what she lacked. The son, unbeknownst to him, will acquire his own and similar insecurities. He will apply what he instinctively *knows* as a father.

When will it end? Does it end? How do such behaviors affect children? To what extent are they prohibited from being or becoming as God intended? Will the son in question become overly attached to his children? Will he be fearful and unable or unwilling to raise independent sons and daughters? Will he understand the value of struggle less?

It is unfortunate what we do to ourselves and others. What we do to our children is doubly troubling. We all fail. Everyone makes mistakes. However, persisting with the ill-advised against sound counsel is unconscionable.

The mother in the illustration rebuffed her husband's admonition. She ignored his request to stop "having hair," as their son called this practice. As a Christian, she defied her husband and church leadership. She sought advice from a secular therapist who opined that such behavior was not inappropriate. We go to great lengths to justify our selfish inclinations, even if we sow seeds of discontent into the souls of our children. This is how we harm ourselves and others.

Not only did the mother deny herself of the possibility of raising a son as God would have her, she deprived her son of healthy mothering God intended. She affected how their son related to his father and defeated how his father raised a son. She rejected her husband's efforts to ensure their son's best interests. How often do we examine the ways we harm our children? Do we consider what we impose upon or deny them?

As I influence Timothy, fundamentals such as truth, experience, independence, contrast, and critical discernment are critical to his well-being. If Timothy is to value his time and relationships and serve a life of purpose, he must appreciate giving and receiving love, the bounty and strength of forgiveness, and the capacity and willingness to respect himself and his fellow man. For him to be strong, wise, and equitable, he must embrace the value of raw experience, which includes tribulation and failure.

If he understands the merits of defeat, he will struggle and do so with purpose and benefit greatly. As he endures suffering and holds firm to his beliefs, he will be blessed. Blessings are bestowed upon sacrifice. He must persevere into blessings.

God anguished over the death of His Son, a loss He could have prevented. Jesus suffered unwanted separation from His Father and then death. When Timothy was upon the ledge, he was separated from his father. By persevering through a cycle of death, we would be reunited, a blessing through sacrifice.

As I assessed Timothy's tribulation upon the ledge, I accounted for his lack, want, need, and blessings. As he braved the unknown, what did he lack? What did he want? What were his needs? How would he be blessed? Did he lack a sense of independence? If so, why? Was he dependent upon someone or something? Was his life so insulated he did not have the ability or heart to persevere? Was his life lived to the exclusion of experiences that were necessary precursors to greater challenges? Was he timid? If he lacked resolve, was it from more than confusion? His choice to leap was critical. To persevere, he had to contend with what was difficult. This was essential.

A boy yearns to emulate his father. A boy sees greatness in his dad. My father was larger than life. When I jumped from the top of the tree trunk, Timothy saw daring resolve. He saw himself in my leap. He wanted to be courageous like me. He wanted to overcome any lack. He wanted to be victorious—to be other than how he was being presently. This desire is inherent within human nature. Consider that children who lack discipline want discipline. We want what we lack and we benefit.

Unfortunately, we often *love* our children to their detriment. A father who pushes his son without understanding the consequences of his harsh parenting does not *love* his child. This is equally true when a father does not allow his son to explore to the point of failure. Are we not expected to bear our burdens? Since God does not allow us to bear more than we are able, should we do any differently with our children? I could do no more and no less than bring Timothy to the point of choosing. Had I done otherwise, he would not have been blessed. Why? Lack. And because of this lack, he needed and wanted to venture into his trepidation and any subsequent blessing.

Consider that:

- The ability to recognize what we lack is critical.
- We may want without realizing our need.
- Needs are perhaps the greatest motivators for struggle.
- We are blessed when we embrace and overcome struggle.

The Ledge
Part Nine

Timothy wanted to jump. Yet, there is a distinction between wanting and knowing he was not willing. Since I was not inclined to force him against his will, recognizing the harm from such short-sightedness, I did what came naturally. I observed until I knew he needed me to come alongside him and then I would provide encouragement.

I stumbled out of the cold water and reached the base of the trail. I grabbed the roots, vines, and branches and leaned into the ascent. My purpose was clear, as clear as the water that could not hide what lay beneath its surface. I would affirm my son and love him as only a father could. I would share my thoughts and he would express those thoughts into action.

When I reached the path that led to the creek behind the mossy ledge, I darted quickly and negotiated the slippery, flat rocks and walked down the middle of the creek bed until I was at Timothy's side. His hair was still wet, but his skin was dry, save a few beads of water that remained on his narrow shoulders. He continued to crouch, not from the cold, but from permanence of inaction, as if chiseled in stone.

As I looked at him, he dropped his arms. It was then that he broke his silence in a way that would move the stoics and embolden the most fervent of fathers. Lifting his blue eyes to mine, he asked, "Why won't my legs do what my mind tells them?" From the mouths of babes, I was amazed at the poignancy of his question. "Oh my, Timothy," I uttered with admiration, "There are men who live fifty and sixty years who never ask such a profound question."

Mind, Emotions, Will, Spirit

Mind – recalling what has been learned; intellectual ability; to
   reason
Emotions – intense feeling; passion; sentiment
Will – a disposition to act according to principles or ends
Spirit – a life-giving force

The mind is a marvelous and amazing creation and with it, we
accomplish great feats. We create, calculate, and construct. The
impact of the heart is as awe inspiring. Emotions are as forceful,
if not more so, and they add meaning to our lives. Whether we
love, laugh, or lament, we feel and express what moves us. The
will channels our thoughts and emotions and serves as the
engine which compels us to act. It drives us to do and to be. The
sum of our thoughts, emotions, and will is the essence of our
souls. Through the soul, we may be all our Creator intended.
Yet, the opposite is true. We may impede possibility and deny
our spirits from communing with God's Spirit.

   Our body is a temporary shell, often referred to as an
instrument or a temple housing the soul and spirit. The body is
the battle ground where the soul and spirit contend with

struggle. If there is no war within the mind, heart, and will, either the soul and spirit are not challenged, as if on autopilot, or they are congruent with God. If we are uninitiated, we do not exercise our will and fail to direct and influence various aspects of our lives. Hence, we do not know and we do not become. A lack of knowledge and understanding leads to our demise. Just as a muscle atrophied by non-use, we fail to exercise the soul and spirit, especially when we confront struggle.

If we critically examined the essence of life, do we not find four elements: thoughts, emotions, action, and being? We act upon thoughts and emotions and this culminates in our being.

Timothy thought, felt, and acted, even if he failed to act. His state of being was based upon how the circumstances occurred to him. He was negative, fearful, and reluctant to be courageous. Given how the scene occurred to him, these were natural responses. Yet, if the situation occurred differently, he could be bold. This was the crux of the matter. Negative thoughts and emotions often govern our existence in this temporal plane. Or when the will is not exercised, we live as automatons, existing, not thriving, not truly engaged.

We are not our thoughts. We are not our emotions. We are not our bodies. Rather, we are the aggregate of what we understand, nothing more and nothing less. Our understanding is derived, in part, from experiences which naturally influence who we become. Our being is directly affected by how we relate with experience. The way we negotiate experiences either hinders or enhances how we relate with ourselves and our capacity to discern and defer to a greater purpose. It is that simple. This simplicity, however, is lost within an intricate web which can be quite convoluted or made so. We may be misguided by our thoughts and emotions to the point of either inaction, a negative state of being, or destruction.

Weigh the following illustration. I know a pastor who is admittedly negative. He believes that the "glass is half empty." He concedes that he is fearful in a negative sense. Surprisingly, he is successful. Given his success, his personal and professional life would be that much more incredible if he possessed the "glass is half full" perspective. What causes a man of fifty-five years to be decidedly pessimistic? What is the source of this predisposition? Are his thoughts and feelings culpable? Why does he fear and couch life with a negative bent? How and why every experience occurs to him contributes to his understanding of himself, his God, and God's will.

As a parallel, consider Timothy standing negatively and reservedly upon the ledge. We observe his mind, heart, and will and begin to fully appreciate why such struggle is formative. Timothy's spirit could feast upon a struggle that would draw him closer to God. This possibility existed. Without this possibility, the reverse occurs. Timothy may know God even less and be as negative in another forty-seven years. He may be reserved, reluctant, and resigned. What will allow him to be more aware and optimistic?

Since Timothy was directly and adversely affected by his thoughts and emotions, his will was equally affected. His being and capacity to act were stymied. How? Why? If another boy his age had come along whistling a tune and lightly negotiated the path and leapt off the ledge without the slightest hesitation, how would we account for such willingness and bravery? There may be any number of answers, but one rings true—understanding. Even if the boy never made this leap before, a positive frame of reference, likely borne from experience, would allow him to govern his soul and act accordingly, with success. He would know himself and be optimistic and bold and, therefore, embrace new experiences with resolve.

Timothy's senses were overwhelmed. He was cold and tense. He was consumed by a fear that gripped his mind and heart. He saw the sights and heard the sounds which altered his intentions. Timothy, a spirit being, was imprisoned within a physical frame. He would not move. Though he had jumped from the tower at the reservoir two months earlier, what he understood from the present situation prevented him from being as he had hoped.

Humanity often overlooks how condemning and defeating the mind can be. While the mind coordinates, creates, and calculates, regrettably, it is adversarial and pessimistic. The mind never stops operating. If we do not arrest its machinations, random thoughts take hold with a heavy influence. "You can't do it!" "You aren't willing!" "Give up before you hurt yourself." We suffer a barrage of negative thoughts that bind or destroy our hopes and initiatives and hinder our abilities.

Recall Timothy's lone question. "Why won't my legs do what my mind tells them?" His mind enslaved him an, as a result, he was immobile. His limited thoughts destroyed any possibility of jumping. He would not leap because he could not leap. This was his *belief.* Yet, since he was not the sum of his thoughts, was he still not able? Was he not more than his perception of all circumstances and limitations. If willing, he could be.

As with his mind, Timothy's heart constrained him. Emotions, the essence of what makes us human, the natural forces within that allow us to feel, the power that gives definition and distinction to what it means to be alive, are as influential as any thought. Emotions spur a father to save a drowning child— love. A man dies within weeks of his wife's passing—sadness. A stranger saves a woman from a careening car—courage.

Emotions move us to do the unthinkable. They move us to do what is right or wrong. Rage kills; anger hurts; love injures. Emotions prevent us from doing what we desire. We fear. Fear may incapacitate a father and prevent him from rescuing his son from peril, a decision which will haunt him for a lifetime.

Remember, Timothy "stood upon a ledge and coaxed himself to jump into the cold clear water eight feet below." "His emotions were conflicting." "He was transfixed by the torrent and turmoil of his emotions and thoughts. He was affected by any number of factors…" The onslaught of negative emotions had an impact. Timothy could not and would not do what he wanted. Whether he was conflicted or confused, his mind and heart were constricted and chaotic.

As emotions controlled his mind and heart, tyranny reigned over this little boy. Persevering through what was easily surmountable became the challenge. Timothy was nothing more than what he understood. What he understood of this battle was based upon his past, a past that distorted his present perspective. While nothing he accomplished previously equalled this experience, his perceptions were a reality that prevented him from knowing.

In the present moment, Timothy's will to act was thoroughly vanquished. Furthermore, the battle would not be won if he was unable to be other than how he everything occurred to himself. Not jumping was a certainty given his present state of being. Was he without the will to be bold? No. He was still *willing*. He was upon the ledge, after all. But he had to overcome how things occurred and the subsequent impact of this occurrence. How was he to reconcile the role of the will his current perception of his circumstances? If Timothy was willing *not* to jump amidst self-doubt or the demands of an unreasonable father, would he still be resolved? Of course. He did not have to jump.

Since Timothy did not reconcile his disparaging thoughts and ominous emotions, his will was caged by how he perceived the situation. Unquestionably, whether he chose to jump or walk away, he would still conquer this tribulation. Either choice would have been courageous. What is the will but a man's capacity to pursue a cause of action, to act volitionally, and accomplish a specific end? The will triumphs or fails to triumph over thoughts and emotions. When faced with the unthinkable, the will asserts. It is the singular influence which spurs action over inaction. Overcoming how circumstances occur requires a *willful decree.*

A willful decree alters what would ultimately culminate in defeat. A willful decree in any struggle is the rite of passage to a new and potentially unfiltered understanding. Timothy would not possess the essence of the struggle upon the ledge without his own willful decree. He had to decree that properly assessing the struggle was of greater value than his present thoughts and emotions. If not, he would remain a victim to his perceptions.

Choosing to willfully decree is not easy; nor should it be. Little of value comes from the uncontested. Moreover, God wants us pressed and molded which happens when we are unsettled. He does not want us satisfied. Willful decrees compel us into discomfort and the unknown. This uncertainty is scary and exciting and foreboding and hopeful.

Timothy wanted a coveted victory. Such a fight would transform and reward him. Since persevering is more valuable than capitulation, a catalyst was needed. Timothy had to willfully decree a transformation. If he did so, and if he overruled his current perceptions, he would triumph over the lies and deceit. If he resolved that neither his thoughts nor his emotions were who he was, he would glory through tribulation. If knowing begets understanding, which begets wisdom, which begets truth, his wilful declaration was critical. If he did not do so, he would remain as he was, which would be outside of possibility.

Since God wants us to be conformed to His image, we must conclude He wants and expects us to endure tribulation. He wants us tested so that our character will be manifested. Character is revealed by and through suffering.

What are obstacles to spiritual understanding? The answer rests partially within how things occur to us. Negative thoughts, maligned emotions, and a lack of will are primary impediments. Growth is further obstructed when we accept these impediments or when we become enamored and fail to act. Regrettably, we fail to experience life to the fullest.

Consider the obvious. If Timothy had not come to the ledge that day, had he stayed home and played video games, he would not have battled what challenged him. The contrast is apparent. Remaining in comfort and abundance would have perpetuated what he knew—convenience and comfort—not pressure. He would not know and experience the unknown and his soul would not have been tested.

Suffering removes us from the immediate and familiar and compels us into randomness and upheaval. This is one of the greatest ironies of life. We arrive at defining understandings when we are unsettled—when we suffer loss. It is then that we become congruent with our spirits.

Consider that:

- The mind is our nemesis; we must control and renew our thoughts.
- While potentially deceptive, emotions are wondrous. Full expression is a marvel.
- A willful decree is the defining act of a warrior who conquers into victory.
- Communing with the divine requires that we command the soul.

The Ledge
Part Ten

Though I approach my children as consistently as possible, Timothy's query humbled me. While all events are instructive, a moment such as this was worthy of a father's influence. With ardent passion, but with the skill of a competent coach, I lowered myself to Timothy's eyes. I explained in simple terms what he confronted. I pointed to the obvious, the noise of the waterfall, the cold water, the ominous appearance of the rocks, the confinement of the trees and cliff that enclosed us. I reminded him of his courage at the reservoir and the valiant jump that was four feet higher. I noted his determination, strength, and ability. I explained that his mind was overwhelmed with conflicting thoughts and strong doubts. I shared that his thoughts and emotions were confused which caused him to fear more than to be bold.

Complicated, Distill, Discernment, Clarity

Complicated – consisting of parts intricately combined; convoluted

Distill – to obtain or purify; clarify, clear

Discernment – the ability to grasp and comprehend; insight; distinguish

Clarity – the quality or state of being clear; lucidity

Life is complicated. We make it so. Yet, if we distilled the essence of life, it would be rather simple. However, distractions abound. We enamor ourselves and this causes confusion. We fail to dignify truth and any clear spiritual purpose. Within a world of confusion, we lack discernment and clarity. If we were earnestly introspective, would we reassess our priorities? Would we question what we value?

Though I always valued my time with Timothy, this moment suddenly acquired distinct meaning. As he battled his thoughts and emotions, I relied upon understanding from my own experiences to affirm him in his present struggle.

Even though he faced what was rather simple, he complicated it.

He was quite incapable of not making this challenge difficult. Such is the downside of inexperience. Such is ruin from confusion. Whether it was this situation or any other, he became fixated and bewildered.

I am not trivializing the act of jettisoning oneself off a ledge. However, during struggles, we often overlook basic elements and conflate other factors until they become overwhelming. When we are unduly affected, the ability to discern is lacking. Clarity is absent. "Timothy! I yelled over the constant clapping of the waterfall. This jump is four feet less than the reservoir!" Note that "He was unaffected... he was transfixed..." "He cared little for my observation." By this point, he wrapped his soul into a pretzel that was pulled tighter with each word of encouragement.

Take a moment and think about Timothy as "he marshalled the gumption to leap." Obviously, the rocks jutting into his consciousness like any three-dimensional image were no idle concern. I was heartened, however, that, by the time I came alongside him, he asked his salient question. "Why won't my legs do what my mind tells them?" Notwithstanding a morass of confusion, he attempted to distill the improbable. He wanted clarity and to discern why he would not willfully decree.

The exchange that followed could not have been more artfully scripted—a boy contending with a quandary sought answers from his father. When Timothy asked a genuine inquiry, I responded definitively. He had clarity. The battle was almost over. The complicated was distilled. Confusion devolved into a clear mandate. He acquired understanding. A father's thought spoken into existence was to be. Timothy and I would do as we resolved.

Noteworthy, what is complicated is often not distilled into clarity for those watching, not at least until after the feat is accomplished. Emma, Maddie, and Holly were without full awareness. Depending upon the relationship with the warrior, some may anguish throughout the tribulation more than others. Emma observed with heavy anticipation. While she faithfully remained in the creek bed, hopeful for her brother's safety and success, she was not privy to the words her father shared. She had an incomplete sense of the struggle. She had a limited appreciation for my intention.

We need only acknowledge the suffering of those at the foot of the cross and the crucifixion of Christ. Mary and the disciples lacked the discernment and clarity of Christ's calling. They were not privy to the words exchanged between Father and Son. No, they persevered as He was inexplicably crucified. Their suffering was excruciating. Yet, in the aftermath of Christ's death, they came to know and understand.

Emma's relationship with me and Timothy, coupled with her separation from us, added to her struggle. She was alone. Holly and Maddie were on the road above the pool of water. It is appropriate, then, to distinguish how people, especially loved ones, are grafted into the heart of struggle. We root for the underdog. We long for warriors to triumph, or we suffer in their loss. Emma would take solace with Timothy's potential victory. She would learn why he struggled so. She would discern and rightly divide what was not known. She, along with her brother, would have clarity.

Consider that:

- The complicated can be made simple.
- In the context of enlightenment, there is nothing worse than confusion.
- When we distill struggle to its inherent simplicity, we discern with clarity.

The Ledge
Part Eleven

I then asked Timothy the only question that mattered. "Do you want to jump?" "Yes," he earnestly replied. I told him he had the will to do so and offered to jump with him. However, I was emphatic. We had to be courageous and choose to act. I explained that, given the slippery rocks, the edge of the ledge was a hazard. We had to be deliberate. We could not doubt. He knew I would not jeopardize his health and well-being with indecision. With a hint of trepidation, Timothy thought for a moment. He then made the choice to jump.

Past, Present, Future, Eternity

Past – having existed or taken place in a period before the
   present
Present – now existing or in progress
Future – coming after the present
Eternity – infinite duration [author's note: an ever present
   present]

Who we are correlates to the present. Our true being has
nothing to do with the past or the future. Timothy had to be
bold, not in the past or the future—he had to be bold now. We
experience life as it unfolds. Being present determines who we
are *presently*. We live genuinely when we are in the present and
not obscured by or anchored in the past. We live in the present
when we are not clouded with future expectations that are
influenced by the past.

   If Timothy lives a life which is not in the present, if he relives
his history, he will be who he has always been. Every tribulation
prepares or fails to prepare him for struggles in some future
present. This point, while potentially confusing, is quite simple.
We cannot live into the past or the future. We live now and only

now—in the present.

This is an important concept. The present is here second by second. The past is gone. The future does not exist. Unfortunately, we bring the past where it does not belong—in the present! Why? The past is what we know. It is familiar and, therefore, comfortable, and acceptable.

Consider one critical thought. When we live in the past, it is always with us. Pointedly, we are shaped and controlled and act or fail to act based upon what once was. This is the rub. Our present understanding should be relevant—not what is *known* of former times. If we accept a dated mental or emotional construct over what is or could be, history is repeated. The present is not created anew.

If Timothy is denied the rigors of struggle, if he denies himself these rigors, he will avoid challenges and live as a timid soul. Tentativeness becomes familiar. This is learned (past) behavior. A sheltered and limited life is the antithesis of a resolve to be strong and courageous. Our limitations manifest a protocol of sorts for a continued existence that is small and uninitiated. This syndrome is largely inescapable. We do not recognize or alter what ails us. By degrees, our lives are governed by prior influences and a world of possibility is denied.

Given the dominance of the heart and mind, we are most authentic when we leave the past in the past. We are more apt to truly be in the unknown if we do not live within two periods at the same time—the present and the past present. In other words, we will *be* if we do not live into a perpetual history. We must embrace the unknown as it happens while spurning reruns of old performances. To be is not the same as been. One may not *been*; yet, one may *be*.

If we are to be in the present, what is known of the past is not relevant. Understanding unfolding and unknown variables is vital. For example, we may *know* 2 + 2 = 4 (the past); yet, we may not know the sum of (2 + P) + (4 + P), with "P" as the variable of possibility. Apply this equation to experience. If we live into the present like a rote formula, we rely upon what we know of the past for any response in the present. Since possibility happens a result of randomness, we neglect the value of randomness and the unknown.

A child who spent the first nine years attached to his mother, a child who lacks a pronounced independence and identity, is the equivalent of:

$$safety + security = present$$

This dynamic *enamors* him with a comfort from his *past present* and shields him from risk in the future *present*. He will less likely grab a vine and swing over a ravine because he *knows* risk aversion—exactly what he learned from his past. The unknown remains unknown. He is not challenged. He does not grow. He does not explore. He does not experience the randomness of life.

Regrettably, people paste the known past where randomness should reign—in the moment—as it arrives. Many fail to appreciate that being in the unknown is exciting, edifying, and glorifying. Being willingly courageous in the unknown requires a present which refutes and or redefines past representations—a transformation which provides awareness and compels us to be other than our history.

The past prevents us from negotiating life in the present with a clean slate. Living in the past projects prejudice. If Timothy lived in comfort and abundance and was insulated from struggle, he would be and remain largely untested. A tendency to avoid struggle may be attributed to the comfort of a past largely free of conflict. Any future present would lack pressure and result in a rather tranquil, linear existence. He would be enamored, avoid pressure, and persevere less. He would reap less character and be less hopeful. With this equation, Timothy would have a shallower understanding of himself. He would know his God even less. He certainly would not know God's will.

Timothy was influenced by his repeated way of being during events in his life that were unrelated to swimming. Timothy was not engaged in the present. When Timothy brought his history forward, he was stifled. His history denied him the possibility of leaping. *His story* was prone to an *already always history*. His story, therefore, would always be present.

I did not care about his past. I did not care about a future which may never exist. Neither the past nor the future was present. Being present is what mattered. Timothy would only accomplish what was possible upon the ledge in the present.

Remember, "I lowered myself to Timothy's eyes. I explained in simple terms what he confronted" (in the present, with his present possibility of being). "I reminded him of his courage at the reservoir (his understanding of being courageous in the past present), and the valiant jump that was four feet higher" (than he presently faced). "I noted his determination (be present), strength (be present), and ability" (be present). "I explained that his mind was overwhelmed with conflicting thoughts and strong doubts" (he lived his known past into the present). I shared that his thoughts and emotions were intertwined into confusion which caused him to fear more than to be bold" (he brought his past to the fore).

The fact that the past denied Timothy the possibility of being and doing something new in the present was a critical thought. If his past reigned supreme, he would not learn from a present full of that was possibility. The opposite would unfold. He would continue to ingrain past precedent. This was tantamount to regurgitating life—rather unappealing except for those satisfied with the status quo. Whether Timothy jumped off the ledge or walked back to the car, he had to be present without interference from the past.

"Do you want to jump?" I asked. His answer mattered little in the sense that he may responded with an underlying *historical* context. However, to shape his being based upon what was imminent, I probed. He would be influenced by what he gleaned from the immediate. How he was being—how he occurred to himself—was more significant than his choice to leap or not. Honestly, he could have said "Yes" and remained a fixture upon the ledge, cemented only by what he knew. In order to defeat this occurrence, Timothy had to reject the past and tap his present ability. If Timothy determined that comfort (enamor) would not impede his understanding, he would persevere.

Timothy's future was only relevant in two respects. The

present may affect any future present and the present and future present influence eternity—a never ending present. If he persevered with a mind, heart, and will focused upon possibility in the present, he would manifest character and hope for eternal blessings. Sequential struggles would lead to greater truth, which would beget further tribulation and even higher truth. Instead of history repeating itself, the present would reveal itself. If eternity is where Timothy receives divine blessings for his obedience and faithfulness, being in the present and leaving the past in the past are essential.

Both struggle and possibility are current and commingled in the present. Timothy had the present possibility to be bold and to do so in the here and now. He had to understand that he could not be bold yesterday or tomorrow. He had to *be* as the present unfolded. What God wants Timothy to experience happens now. Who God wants him to be happens now. He makes me proud now. He glorifies God now. We hope for eternity now. If Timothy conquered the struggle upon the ledge in the present, he would understand how to overcome future trials as they occur—in the present.

Consider that:

- We should not bring the past into the present.
- We may only *be* in the present.
- The future does not exist.
- Our spirits yearn for eternity—an ever-expanding present.

The Ledge
Part Twelve

We determined that on the count of three, we would leap. Yet, on three, Timothy was as immovable as he was for the last fifteen minutes. We both looked at each other and started laughing. The comic relief was unexpected, but welcomed. I then encouraged him to reconsider. "No!" he said. He was resolved. This time I clasped his hand. I looked into his eyes and said, "We are going to jump on three." Timothy nodded in agreement. "What do I always tell you, Timothy?" "Trust Daddy," he replied. "One, two, three!"

Dependence, Independence,
Interdependence, Trust

Dependence – reliance, trust; something on which one relies
Independence – autonomy, freedom, not subject to control
Interdependence – dependence upon another
Trust – assured reliance on the character, strength or truth of
    someone

Suffering is integral to dependence, independence, and
interdependence. Suffering is integral to trust. Dependence,
independence, and interdependence are qualities based upon
trust and are crucial for relationships and life. Dependence
implies the need and support of another—reliance. Our children
depend upon us. We do not love them if we fail to raise
independent children. Love requires that we let them go and
allow for their eventual autonomy. This act breeds trust.

Independence is encouraged early in life and acquired over time.
We value independence. We want to be independent. However,
independence is not an end all. Moreover, independence
complements interdependence. A failure to be autonomous is an
obstacle to interdependence and leads to distrust.

I want my children to experience failure. I want them to struggle. Since adversity will happen anyway, why not invite tribulation with a healthy context and grounded attitude? Wholesome struggle breeds self-sufficiency; otherwise, seeds of insecurity are sown early in life. Unhealthy dependence digs deep, metastasizes, and forms maligned conditions. The reverse is true when a child suffers forced independence by deprivation. He becomes a hollow shell. He becomes angry and rejects goodwill because he does not know love. His *independence* is harsh and lonely. He hides behind a hardened exterior and craves a constructive dependence he never had. The contrast between ultra-dependence and ultra-independence is stark.

But for a reluctance to prune them, children become an extension or repulsion of their fathers and mothers. This occurs when parents insulate or deprive their children to a fault. Undue attachment to what is comfortable and known inhibits healthy mental, emotional, and spiritual growth, each of which is essential for independence. Hyper or deprived dependence instills profound weakness. When we fail to struggle or reject struggle, whether in a state of dependence, independence, or interdependence, we are ill-prepared and ill-equipped.

True dependence lasts but a season. Timothy's dependence upon me during childhood has a practical and definitive end. Yet, out of a sense of love and belonging, he will seek mutual dependence in some future present. Independence draws us back to dependence. One reason for this dynamic is humanity's common conditioning from suffering. Suffering is a part of life's curriculum—a core requirement. Through and with tribulation, we bring understanding and strength back to family and community.

Consider the following two choices. Would you prefer to live a life of relative ease or one fraught with challenges? As his father, I do not want Timothy to live a life of comfort. I wanted my son to persevere upon the ledge. I want him to persevere upon all of life's ledges. I want him to persevere through suffering.

Since dependence is prerequisite for confidence and subsequent independence, Timothy's struggle upon the ledge was opportune. He could follow my lead—dependence. Children mirror a father's behavior. They emulate their parents hoping to be larger than life. This is an instinctive aspiration. If we denigrate this drive, children will struggle needlessly and aimlessly or they will not struggle at all. They will not appreciate full independence and lack confidence. They will not trust.

Trust becomes a critical element. "What do I always tell you, Timothy?" is the question I asked my son. "Trust Daddy!" he replied. I wanted him to trust—a trust which comes only with a confident dependence, as well as a sure independence and interdependence. My son trusted me. He knew I sought his best interests. I instilled confidence, not suspicion. His dependence upon my counsel and actions was essential.

While I believed Timothy might leap on his own accord, his dependence upon me was appropriate. This struggle was but one in a life-long series from which he would grow stronger and wiser. Tribulation is essential. Tribulation produces. Timothy's dependence will breed independence and bring him back to dependence and interdependence from a trust underscored by struggle.

While a man will always be his own to whatever extent, he will value and need the company, counsel, and concern of others. The spiritual truth of mutual interdependence occurs when we realize the value of relationships. My son needed me. Did he exhibit the independence I had hoped? I had no expectations. This was a challenge unlike any other. Appropriately, through this experience, Timothy was dependent, independent, interdependent, and trusting.

Timothy was dependent upon me as he learned what he lacked and, with a sense of independence, he chose to act. With his consent, he and I became interdependent. My son trusted at each phase of the endeavor. Remember, "I clasped his hand." Interdependence. "I looked him in the eyes and said, 'We are going to jump on three.' He nodded in agreement." Trust. He wanted to persevere dependently, independently, and interdependently, and would do so trustingly.

When the day arrives when I am no longer in Timothy's life, my hope is that he will battle fiercely and wisely with the known and unknown. I have a hope that he will be transformed from dependence to independence and interdependence with a profound and uncompromising trust. May he draw upon his own integrity and ability and those of his compatriots as he knows and trusts in God's sovereign will.

Consider that:

- Dependence lasts but a season, notwithstanding that we are always dependent upon community.
- Independence is required for daring resolve.

- Interdependence is a natural component of any warrior's perseverance into possibility.
- Trust is the foundation of all relationships and affords us increased blessings from struggle.

The Ledge
Part Thirteen

As I leaped off the ledge, I could not help but notice my arm was fully extended and there was tension between me and Timothy that should not have been. For an instant, I was airborne while he was still held captive to the ledge and his own limitations. I was not going to release my hand. Inevitably, Timothy's frozen frame was freed from that formidable foe waging the brunt of this battle. Two warriors, father and son, were free-falling into the unknown. Two warriors embraced one of the many random variables of possibility manifested in and through struggle.

Observe, Question, Reconcile, Surrender

Observe – to see or sense through careful attention
Question – to ask; to subject to analysis
Reconcile – to bring to submission or acceptance
Surrender – to yield; to give up completely or agree to forgo

The power of observation is often neglected, which is one reason we are blind to our circumstances. The ability to observe is an asset like any other skill and it needs to be exercised. Yet, the reverse is also true. We may observe to a fault, which is referred to as paralysis by analysis, and fail to act. Paralysis renders us unable or unwilling to do as hoped. Or, we may observe incorrectly and weigh a particular aspect of a situation over others. This culminates in an imbalance, a prejudice, or predisposition with a tendency to do one thing over the alternative.

Timothy was paralyzed. He was prejudiced. He heeded certain aspects of the jump more than others. He was, therefore, inert and would not likely change his outlook. What was he observing? Why? What affected his intention to jump? "His mind was plying its trade of deceit and doubt." Based upon what and how he observed, Timothy's mind, heart, and will were adversely affected. This is what I observed. Timothy had to understand how and why he impeded himself. Awareness requires objective observation. Observations are not lucid when foreboding thoughts and emotions are pressing.

A child fixated upon a wasp will not open a window. A child plowed by fear will not look under the bed for monsters which do not exist. When enraged, we fail to love. We are held captive to limiting thoughts and emotions and refuse to consider other possibilities. Timothy was not receptive to my observations. Was he moved by the thought that this leap from upon the ledge was four feet less than the platform? No. His mind was bound and his emotions were not only trapped, but churning. He was predisposed to limitations, not possibilities.

In order to see the unseen, Timothy had to be aware. This meant he had to discount what obscured his mind and heart. To accept an alternative perspective, he needed clarity. He had to observe things as they were, not as he perceived them. "I lowered myself to Timothy's eyes and explained in simple terms what he confronted. I reminded him of his courage at the reservoir, of the valiant jump that was four feet higher." It was then that "I pointed to the obvious…" I underscored what prevented him from acquiring proper context.

He had to understand the reasons that he was immovable. "I noted his determination, strength, and ability." Observation. "I explained that his mind was overwhelmed with conflicting thoughts and strong doubts." Observation. There was a struggle within this boy. Observation. He was not willing to jump.

Observation. When I asked, "Do you want to jump?" he replied positively. Then "I told him he had the will to do so and offered to jump with him." He had to question his own understanding.

The path to objective observation is through the power of questions. Consider this creed: *He who asks questions has control.* Is this not true? Are you able to disprove this creed? What is your explanation? Do you appreciate the power of queries? Does the one asking questions not have control?

For Timothy to observe, he had to, as if employing the scientific method, critically question his predicament. He had to challenge what he knew. Do we not have an already forecasted representation? Yes. Timothy had to dislodge, unsettle, and reject the notions which bound him. What did he do? He asked the most salient question. "Why won't my legs do what my mind tells them?" He was in control.

With this query, he made the most important observation of all. He searched for the reason why he was not being bold. He genuinely wanted to understand. With an appropriate answer, he would solve the riddle and dispel a grave misunderstanding— how the struggle occurred to him.

Timothy paused. He probed. His searched for the truth over the lie. Would he extinguish doubt? Would he dispense with the confusion? Would he offer a solution? Would he willfully decree? Would he ask the questions Who? What? When? Where? Why? How? and reconcile what affected him? If he did, he would understand these circumstances surrounding him and surrender to a battle he did not need to fight. For, it was a battle he could not win.

Reconciliation is not easy; surrender often is. Reconciliation is a concession which must eventually be granted while surrender is demanded. Often a choice to surrender leads to victory. Why is this so? When one surrenders, he accepts conditions that are interminable. This fact is defining. Unalterable conditions are inconsequential to struggle and unworthy of a warrior's attention or efforts.

I often surrendered to my brother's size and brute strength when he tackled me to the ground. I had no reason to reconcile. I had no concessions to make. Surrender was appropriate. The circumstances were as they would be. I made a choice to accept them. Acquiescing to a superior force was wise and practical and lessened potential repercussions.

Timothy could not change the circumstances—the noise, temperature, sights—that caused mental and emotional tumult. Timothy had but one choice. Just as if he were thirsty and had only mineral water, or if he received one gift on his birthday, he must choose to accept each. To miss this point is to reject a profound path toward the world of possibility. Regardless of his course of action, Timothy had to accept the circumstances in and around him. He had to choose to be bold.

General Thomas "Stonewall" Jackson stated, "You may be whatever you resolve to be." Resolve separates those who will be from those who will not. It is that simple. If Timothy resolved to overcome what impeded him from being bold, he would surrender. He would resolve to be bold knowing circumstances affecting his mind and heart would never change. Surrender. Surrender and step boldly into the storm. Walk straight into the deceit and doubt and declare a willful decree. The choice was clear.

When I "encouraged him to reconsider," he was emphatic. "No!" he said. Picture what followed. When I stated that we would jump on three, my son looked at me and "nodded in agreement." The unstated spoke volumes. His resolve awed the trees, birds, water, and mist. The waterfall hushed momentarily. Timothy chose to surrender. He saw the circumstances for what they were—mere distractions. He could not have prevailed otherwise. Of greater import, he had no cause to battle. The natural will do as it naturally does. He now understood and resolved to venture into raw possibility.

When we surrender, we cease any compunction to control. This is wisdom. Deceit and doubt are vanquished when we are freed from binding thoughts and emotions. We see around, through, and over the confusion. While the fear may not subside, our resolve is seemingly ordained. Surrender is final.

Timothy surrendered. He chose to willfully decree and resolved to decree completely. His character would be wrought as he persevered into possibility. As we formed our father and son pact and chose to act, he would reap blessings.

Consider that:

- We must exercise the power of observation.
- He who asks questions has control.
- Reconciliation is good for the soul.
- Surrendering is an act of relinquishing control and ceasing futile effort.

The Ledge
Part Fourteen

The inevitable became a reality. Timothy and I descended and plunged into the pool. When we surfaced, I rejoiced in his bravery. "Yahoo!" I exclaimed, as Holly, Maddie, and Emma cheered. "You did it!"

After we swam to shallow waters, I pulled him close and hugged him. "I am so proud of you, Timothy." Surprisingly, not wanting any credit, he looked at me with humility and innocence and said, "I didn't jump, Daddy. You pulled me in." Yet, Timothy did everything he needed to prevail. Little did he know the wealth of understanding he had acquired.

I looked at my son, who was now united with his father in victory, and unquestioningly affirmed that he leapt off the ledge. I underscored that we did it together. He braved tribulation with perseverance which revealed his character and gave him hope. Timothy, to whatever small degree, came to know and understand himself that much more. With yet another tribulation, Timothy came that much closer to knowing himself, God, and His will.

Thought, Word, Sacrifice, Love

Thought – conception; idea, opinion, belief; product of thinking
Word – a declaration that one will do or refrain from doing;
    expression
Sacrifice – to accept the loss or destruction of for an end; cause
    or ideal
Love – unselfish, loyal and benevolent concern for others

A man is as he understands. If he understands his situation as
fearful, he is intimidated. Since the mind is held captive to one
thought at a time, the ability to govern thought is crucial. This is
exactly why I detest the word *can't*. I am intolerant of the idea
my children would consider themselves unable or unworthy.
Such thoughts compel me to be decidedly positive simply to
counter the impact. I believe in my children, why shouldn't they
believe in themselves?

    Since Timothy was what he understood, I encouraged him to
be bold. I countered his pessimism and shared it was not what
happened to him that was important; rather, what he *understood*
about what happened to him was critical. How Timothy
expressed his thoughts, both verbally and by action, was

fundamental. If he controlled and fully expressed his thoughts, nothing would unduly influence him.

When asked who He was, did God not say, "... I AM"?[5] God is the source of all, the creative wellspring, the one, true consciousness. God, as the great I AM, is complete awareness and presence. God is thought. From His thought, we have the Word. Who is the Word? His Son, the Christ, who is nothing less than worthy. Timothy is my son. He is worthy. He creates thought. He is word. He is I am.

Timothy's thoughts were paramount upon the ledge. His thoughts were greater than all circumstances. His thoughts were the creative impetus to a willful decree. He would not prevail without optimistic thoughts and truth. His belief that he was worthy and capable was essential. To create this transformation, he had to express these thoughts with words.

No word occurs without a thought. The two are inseparable. Timothy's inaction resulted from a battle between his thoughts and expressions. He asked, "Why won't my legs do what my mind tells them?" This thought bound his legs. He had to choose a different thought and transform himself by word so he could be *I am*. He had to express his thoughts and be in a world of possibility, not one of limitations. Emerson said, "What you are preaches so loudly that I cannot hear what you say."[6] Timothy had to be bold. With new thoughts, his words would scale with his intent.

Timothy had to *be* and this required sacrifice. Timothy would not leap—sacrifice—if his thoughts were discordant with his intent. Since no one could force him to think or be any differently, he had to reject the lie and accept the truth. He had to speak truth into existence, an act that would culminate in possibility. Timothy had to exchange *can't* for *can*, *won't* for *will*, and *unable* for *able*. He had to express his words through action. He had to sacrifice the safety and security he valued. What he prized most denied him of a higher priority—his intention to do what he was able.

Timothy had to relinquish what was comfortable and venture into the unknown. Is this not sacrifice? This was not an easy feat for this eight-year-old boy. He coveted the comfort (a thought) of staying upon the ledge. He wanted to remain (an act) upon the ledge. Sacrifice was required in order to turn defeat into victory. This is one of the most unorthodox principles of life. We do not think of gaining through defeat.

The irony is that we gain through loss. As an act of love, faith, and obedience, whether for himself, his father, or his God, Timothy had to sacrifice. Sacrifice required him to relinquish control. Timothy had to surrender. Concession is good for the soul. Akin to planting and harvesting, bounty from sacrifice is inevitable. If he accomplished what his father knew he could, he would reap what was sown in adversity and possess a hope commensurate with his perseverance.

Recall that "I noted his determination, strength, and ability." This thought, spoken by words, was essential for success. He knew of my confidence in him. With my affirmation, I countered his negative and judgmental thoughts. He had to think differently and defy his perceived safety. Sacrificing while he faced his fears would enable him to be bold.

The conclusion? Being in and with unknown possibilities by

and through struggle allows one to know himself, God, and His will. We were created in God's image. God understands the value of struggle. He orders or allows tribulation for our benefit and His glory. God seeks our good, not harm. When we understand who we become by and through times of testing, when we rightly discern tribulation, we inherently defer to a Creator who knows what we need. Do we, then, not know Him and His character better? We certainly may not presume God does not know about suffering. The loss of His Son was personal and significant.

Moreover, how God responds to loss and suffering is noteworthy. His varied responses in scripture, from compassion to accountability, reflect a God who is sensitive toward trials. God understands our desperate need. He knows we seek Him through and because of tribulation. Tribulation draws us closer to a God who wants to relate with us. Our dependency, a natural consequence of adversity, brings us before a God who provides.

Discerning God's will is no different. As we are drawn to God, what do we see but His nature? We see a loving, merciful, just, possessive, strong, forgiving, and generous God. We see a God who is our perfect example. We see who we may be. Our mandate is to reflect His divine nature. If we become Christ-like through our sufferings, we glorify God. Tribulation provides a departure from our former selves. As we morph into new creations, we become as He intended.

Whether we know God's will generally or specifically, we may reckon our understanding with confidence. Herein rests a benefit of tribulation. We are brought to a point of resignation. With resignation, our lives become a testament to God and His divine will. We understand that we are not our own. We are spiritual beings longing for an intimate and truth-filled relationship with Him. God's priorities become our priorities. We need only express Christ's words, "Father, if you are willing, take this cup from me; yet not my will, but yours be done."[7] Suffering bring us to this sacrificial dependence.

The brief explanation of knowing God and His will under the section that deals with *Thought, Word, Sacrifice*, and *Love* is appropriate. This chapter began with, "A man is as he understands." With and through a man's words and actions, by sacrifice, as the pestle of tribulation grinds him within the mortar of life, he may come to know God and His truth. We may extrapolate that, through a life of trials, Timothy will reach this noble aim. The struggle upon the ledge, a trial he endured with his earthly father, was a direct parallel of what he endured with his heavenly Father. May he reckon this understanding through every struggle and hope for divine revelation.

Consider that:

- Our thoughts are greater than all circumstances. Who we understand ourselves to be is who we are.
- Our words—full expression—lead to transformation. We have the capacity to speak victory into existence.
- We gain through sacrifice. We prosper in defeat.
- Love mandates that we suffer and allow others to persevere through struggle.

The Ledge
Part Fifteen

As we made our way to the edge of the creek, I watched my son. He beamed. Yes, something happened that day. Timothy encountered the unknown and, as a result, came to know himself more. God created my son to conquer a ledge and enter a world of possibility. God created me to shepherd my son through dark valleys and Timothy would receive much by persevering through struggle. Such is victory.

When we reached Holly and Maddie, we celebrated. We took satisfaction as witnesses of a boy who battled into victory. Emma admired her brother. Her mind and heart attested to a feat which taught her about his character. Timothy grew immeasurably in her estimation. Whether she realized it or not, Emma was inspired by the manifestation of Timothy being in and battling through tribulation. Emma, Holly, Maddie, and I want, need, and depend upon the resolve of warriors like Timothy, those who dare to venture where many fear to tread.

When we continued our trip to the river, I looked at Timothy. He sat with his hands upon his lap. His countenance reflected both contemplation and joy. His face revealed the hint of a grin which he fought to hide as his eyes glanced to those dear. Timothy could not have adequately expressed what he thought and felt about his victory. He was proud in a humble and satisfying sense. I knew that he knew he had accomplished the unthinkable. I was grateful for my son's growth through a defining tribulation. He was a conquering warrior.

Whether for my son's courageous being from the unknown into understanding, or my choice to affirm a boy as he becomes the man God intends, I took solace in the love I felt. I took quiet satisfaction as I admired the wonder, beauty, and bounty realized in and through tribulation. Timothy and Emma grew that day. This, to me, was the epitome of fatherhood—the affirmation of my children. I proclaimed, "It is good." God was glorified. With the sweet aroma of sacrifice—the pinnacle act of worship of a boy who honored both his earthly and heavenly fathers through tribulation—God was satisfied that it was good. Timothy came to know himself, his God, and God's will by perseverance into character and a hope that will not disappoint.

Broken, Revelation, Oneness, Worship

Broken – shattered; subdued; crushed

Revelation – something revealed; an enlightening or astonishing disclosure

Oneness – a single person or thing

Worship – to regard with respect, honor or devotion

Brokenness is a state of being that often involves desperateness and hopelessness. One who is broken is humbled by despair. He is mentally drained, emotionally spent, and physically exhausted. Life is truly empty and meaningless. This cycle reaches its darkest when death has greater appeal than life.

Why would anyone want someone else to be broken? Why would a father wish his son to endure the imponderable? If his son were broken, a father would want him to persevere, to acquire the character commensurate with this desperate state of being. He would want him to become stronger and wiser.

Why did God allow His Son to be broken? Christ had a purpose. He persevered into a hope and accomplished His Father's will. Christ anguished. Not wanting the tribulation, He asked the burden be taken from Him. He loathed the idea of separation from God. Christ wrestled with grave thoughts, emotions, and physical agony, all from His obedience to His Father's will. Yet, His suffering and eventual brokenness were not for naught. Did Christ not defeat sin and death?

As He prayed alone in the quiet of the garden, his disciples slept. His anguish was great. He sweated blood from His brow. Imagine bearing the sins of humanity without support. He was alone, betrayed, and rejected. His plight became even more solitary. His disciples scattered. Peter denied him thrice. Beaten and scorned, He was crucified. Brokenness.

Only a man of perseverance and character could suffer so great a tribulation and be victorious. A broken man will hopefully discern. In such a state of brokenness, is it not better to seek and know God's will, glorify His name, and worship Him? Undoubtedly, God uses brokenness to achieve this end.

Something raw and credible, something transformative occurs when a man is broken and he rightly discerns. With no escape, he is foursquare with truth. Life becomes empty and meaningless. The divine becomes an end all. Death is no longer a foe. Life and all its trappings are seen as shallow and hollow. When one is broken through life-defining suffering and he discerns, he surrenders. He sacrifices as a testament to his Creator. He reconciles that he is redeemed and his life is not his own. This is no trifle revelation. A broken and discerning man seeks union with God and accepts that there is nothing else.

While Timothy was not broken upon the ledge, he endured one of the many trials which would break him in some small measure. Future tribulation will mold him. He will be defined, refined, and prepared for even greater trials. If ever truly broken, may he weather all and surrender into a bleakness where even hope is fleeting. Why? Revelation. In a state of brokenness, we gain the most transformative insight. Our vulnerability is fully exposed. We understand that we can affect nothing. We accept a need for absolute dependence—oneness. When a man has nothing left and nothing upon which to hope, he is wholly resigned to what may and will be.

Timothy depended upon me. He wanted to be reunited, to be one with his father. I provided revelation. Revelation offered him hope. Timothy wanted to be bold and victorious. He wanted my acclaim and admiration. Did he sweat blood? Was he racked in physical pain? Not even close. But he struggled and came to appreciate his limitations. Tribulation brought him to a greater intimacy with himself and his father. Oneness. Our integrity as father and son strengthened. We became fellow warriors. We climbed the trail together. We reached the ledge hand in hand. We determined to leap as one. We struggled as one. We hoped as one.

After my leap, I waited. I championed his calling. I encouraged a son who hoped to accomplish and honor his father's will. Timothy wanted victory and I wanted him to succeed. From my perspective, his victory was in his death. When he balked, I noticed and admired the ensuing battle.

Life-defining events strengthen the integrity of the soul. Integrity is more than honor; it means completeness and wholeness. A foundation is not complete and is without integrity if there is no cornerstone. A cornerstone is not whole if it is not square. A bicycle wheel is not whole or complete with a broken spoke. With every battle, Timothy will be pressed into congruency with his true self—his character and the integrity of his being.

Herein rests the bounty of suffering in and through brokenness. We are drawn to God as we better understand ourselves as a result of tribulation. When we acknowledge our inadequacies, we depend upon Him. When we honor and obey God's will, life becomes defining. As we possess this truth, we perform the greatest act of worship. We become like Christ, for "to live is Christ… to die is gain."[8] We become one with Him.

Do we have any higher calling? Worship, reverent devotion for our Creator, is never more significant than when we know we were bought with a price. We are to be spent at a cost to the praise of His name regardless of the circumstances. We were not created to live as denizens of this world, enamored within the distorted, desensitized to a lack of appreciation of our weaknesses and need for God. This is the essential contrast. If we fail to understand the value of struggle, we thwart the possibility of knowing ourselves and God. We fail to worship. Struggle, if rightly discerned, purges the soul of confusion so that we may honor and glorify God.

Absent tribulation, waywardness and confusion reign. We instinctively treasure comfort over randomness. We prize abundance over sacrifice. We covet tranquility over tumult, serenity over strife, self over spirit, disunity of spirit with the Spirit of God. What is our calling? What is our divine purpose? Is it to know God and to seek and do His will?

How do we achieve this end? Tribulation produces. If we understand suffering by persevering into character, subsequent hope will not disappoint. As tribulation reveals our true identities, as we become congruent with God through struggle, we take joy in His nature and will. We surrender into oneness. This is integrity. Christ sought oneness with His Father. He sought God's will even at the expense of His life. Worship.

Timothy desired to be one with me. He did not want to be separated. He hoped to triumph and declare his worth as a warrior. Struggle reveals the possibility to be one with and to honor his father and God.

God alone knows if Timothy will ever be broken. If this occurs, may he be prepared; may his prior struggles serve him well; may he have the character to persevere into understanding, wisdom, and truth. Given the brevity of life and the import of God's leading, brokenness is a direct path to the revelation of His will.

Struggle. Struggle and be bold. Decree into a hope beyond understanding and die into truth.

Consider that:

- Brokenness often avails the greatest insight.
- Revelation draws one out of despair and into hope.
- There is no more defining ideal than to be *one* with those we love.
- As the created, we are called to offer our lives as a testament—an act of worship—to the Creator.

Convergence

As I reflect upon Timothy's struggle upon the ledge, I am humbled. He was afforded the possibility to *be*. The satisfaction of knowing Timothy persevered underscores the inherent worth of fathers and the bounty and wonder of struggle. Emma's courageous jump from the concrete platform at the reservoir reflects this sentiment. The boldness, trust, and love she exhibited are a marvel. You may view her valiant jump on our Youtube channel. Search for "temmathy333" or use this link: https://www.youtube.com/watch?v=oLM1LJpOnZc.

Emma contended with struggle and lived into possibility. Her triumph and Timothy's victory underscore that the love and trust between a father and his children are bonds forged in and by tribulation. Oneness.

In the end, before we leave this temporal plane, may we acknowledge that we contend with more than the obvious. We battle challenges which confront us from our first breath. Tribulation is a constant in life. Moreover, struggle is often a spiritual battle we cannot see. With this divine perspective, I seek to affirm my children. If I accomplish this solemn responsibility, they will negotiate life in a manner more glorifying to God than the alternative. The reason should be apparent. If they persevere into tribulation with the character that naturally ensues, they will have a hope as they know themselves, their God, and His will even more. Tribulation produces.

Imagine being incarcerated for a crime you did not commit, or separated from your son and daughter for years. More importantly, weigh the implications upon your children as they suffer from your absence. This was my plight. Not only does struggle reveal a divine decree, it maintains the integrity of life. Tribulation serves as an elastic agent and pulls humanity back to the essential fundamentals of being. Irony.

As I examine my unjust incarceration, it is difficult to reconcile the suffering of other innocent men in prison—victims of corrupt government practices and the American *justice* system. America is now the most incarcerated country in the world. The number of people trapped by overzealous federal and state prosecutors and power-hungry bureaucrats has escalated beyond any reasoned explanation. The net result is unfathomable suffering for imprisoned men and women and their families.

I was imprisoned with a man who was unjustly convicted. He had already served six years of a fifteen-year sentence. His only son was two years old when he was incarcerated. Another innocent man was in his sixth year of a fifteen-year sentence for bank fraud he never committed. In a post-conviction review, an independent financial forensic auditor cleared him of any wrong doing. Yet, he still fights for justice and exoneration while his six-year-old son is effectively without a father.

Both men stand upon the ledge. They believe in God as each

seeks understanding for His will with such loss. Each has the intent to persevere. What is the source of their willingness to persevere into character if not hope? What do these men possess if not truth? Is there something else? Since tribulation is an element of humanity that compels men to endure, even if they do not prevail into victory, they are drawn to greater dependence upon God. Let there be no doubt, if struggle never culminates in victory, if we suffer the most egregious conditions, God and truth remain absolute.

My friends in prison combatted the inconceivable. This one trait underscores the elasticity of struggle. Each man is drawn back to the basic elements of life that define their beings. The effects of tribulation are not unlike gravity. But for the gravitational pull that keeps us grounded, life as we know it would be torn asunder. Such is the impact of struggle and the power of hope.

Who has not witnessed a spoiled child or an apathetic adult? Those who are not refined by the heat of battle are rarely centered. It is as if they ignore the very laws that bind the essence of life as one. Without character, they have little hope. They will not persevere. Their thoughts and emotions are not tethered. They exist by impulse or whims. Their existence defies purpose. Their lives epitomize the antithesis of struggle. Irony. Contrast.

Appropriately for those who persevere, God becomes a refuge. He is truth. Faith in Him, especially through tribulation, is defining. We are His sons and daughters standing upon the ledges of life. God hopes for our dependence. If we appreciate tribulation, we may distill our need and want for God. We may now Him as Abba, Father. We know His will. He wants to mold us into His nature for our benefit and for His purpose and glory. This will not happen absent struggle. Tribulation produces.

There can be but one salient point to be gained from this discussion. Our heavenly Father affirms us as we persevere through the unknown and all that is possible through struggle. This thought provides peace beyond understanding. Peace gained through faith in God's sovereign will provides solace.

Timothy had a peace about and through him as he persevered with his struggle upon the ledge. Otherwise, he would have left the moment he arrived. The peace he experienced during and afterward was directly attributable to a father's affirmation. Struggle drew him to essential elements of being and he depended upon me for these fundamentals. Such is the affirmation of children. He yearned for that dependence. Timothy had the faith to persevere into victory for his benefit and his father's glory. The precursor to Romans 5: 3-5 aptly establishes this important point.

> Therefore, since we have been justified through faith, we have peace with God through our Lord Jesus Christ, through whom we have gained access by faith into this grace in which we now stand. And we boast in the hope of the glory of God. [9]

Faith is the "confidence in what we hope for and assurance about what we do not see."[10] What did Timothy do? He hoped. He hoped for the substance of things he could not see. Timothy could not see what his father saw. Yet, he had faith. The two men unjustly imprisoned may not see what God has ordained; however, they manifest a faith that provides a peace regardless of the circumstances and the outcome. They hope. This hope affirms even when faith is questioned and hope is fleeting.

Consider God's satisfaction as we weather storms. As I walked with Timothy, as he persevered upon the ledge, God was there. We need only maintain our faith that, amid trials which try men's souls, God grieves as our spirits grieve. During our darkest hours, we run to our fathers, both heavenly and earthly. But, at times, we still do not listen. We may hear sage counsel, but we do not honor the message. Even if Timothy did not listen, *I knew* he could prevail.

As we strive with futility, quite often lacking wisdom, we invariably accomplish what is in vain. This is when God patiently abides, knowing we will eventually come to the end of ourselves. Death. It is then that we cease our self-effort. It is then that we surrender, as if we capitulate when God whispers His gentle appeal to "Trust Daddy." We trust with a faith which perseveres into character and hope. Yes, tribulation produces.

When in a fierce struggle, when suffering, when unjustly hauled away to prison, I can hear my Father encourage me to walk directly into the heart of suffering. "Ignore the sights and sounds, my son," He declares. "Do not fret about what you are unable to affect." This is when God reassuringly says, "Trust me while you fight for truth and justice. Timothy and Emma are in my care." God knows I have been broken. It was then that He wept for and with me. "You have the heart for truth, son, and, therefore, you have traveled this path. You have a heart for equity, son. Those who condemn you do not understand." He appreciates that not knowing ails me. "You cannot know, precious child. Thus, you are a warrior. Stand upon the ledge and know I am. Behold My glory through your faith. This is My will."

There is a moment in many a battle when the tide turns. The momentum shifts. This is when all of creation notes the marked change in a warrior's soul and spirit. Nature is held in abeyance. Like a mighty wind, the force of one's surrender traverses into the spiritual. The soul relinquishes and the warrior's spirit reckons the truth. He reckons God's will. "I have a plan for you, son. My plan is for your benefit and My glory." The warrior no longer views his life from the context of the immediate. He has an eternal frame of reference. "You belong to me, my son. Leap from upon the ledge and *know* I am God."

Epilogue

Many years from now when I am in a season of life filled with fond memories, when my grey hair and wrinkled face disclose the age of my slowing body and feeble walk, I hope to visit both the platform and the ledge. Perhaps Cory, Heather, Timothy, Emma, and their children will accompany me. I would like to tell my grandchildren of mighty feats and conquering warriors. I hope to witness my sons and daughters encourage and shepherd young souls into the heart of struggle. It would be an honor and distinct privilege to see the cycles of life unfold in my progeny. I would be humbled by the fruit produced after years of affirming my children as they shape their children into God-fearing, God-knowing warriors.

Like salmon returning to their place of spawning, I want to take the road we traveled after Timothy leapt off the ledge. This tree-lined road parallels the mighty Shenandoah and curves sharply to the left. There that a path meanders to the right and down to the river's edge. This scene is as beautiful as any. The water rolls deeply and gently and spills effortlessly over a low-lying barrier of rocks which accents a crooked line of rapids stretching across the width of the river. The fish feed underneath these shallow rapids. The water flows past a bend some two hundred yards to the right where a tall sycamore stands majestically. The largest limb stretches out from the shore and over the river. Two bald eagles sit atop this limb and look toward the fish-filled rapids.

When ready, the eagles take flight. They descend and fly a foot above the surface and then glide stealthily northward. Suddenly, they extend their talons into the water and seize their unsuspecting prey. While the fish twists to and fro, the eagle flap its wings and ascends to a nearby tree and devours the catch. Below, wild flowers adorn the banks and reveal the end of a long summer. They droop with age and when the early fall breeze blows, their petals shift and seeds loosen and drop into the fertile soil. Cycles.

Yes, within this venue, I want mothers and fathers and innocent and eager children to catch crawfish and skip rocks with an old warrior. I hope we cast fishing lines into the rapids and my grandchildren squeal with delight when floats disappear and poles bend. I aspire to laugh with joy and live into a world of possibility with those I love. Oneness.

These were my thoughts when I was confined behind a fourteen-foot steel fence lined with four rolls of concertina wire. Twenty years hence, I will have greater insight as to why my children and I suffered separation for years. By then God may have imparted His higher purpose and, if not, I will take quiet confidence, even then, that His will was and will be done.

Just as the cycles of life continue, as eagles raise eaglets to fly and survive, as flowers perpetually pepper the landscape with seeds, as fish lay eggs and search for food in shifting currents, as seasons change from gentle spring to harshness of winter, and as man braves every ledge imaginable, may we know ourselves and abide with an obedience, faith, perseverance, character, and hope that is a revelation of God and His will. Life is far too brief and valuable to shun the virtue of what tribulation produces.

There is a verse that is timely and appropriate for wherever we may find ourselves. It reflects the core of a father's purpose.

> And the God of all grace, who called you to his eternal glory in Christ, after you have suffered a little while, will Himself restore you and make you strong, firm and steadfast.[11]

Strong, firm, and steadfast. Perseverance, character, and hope. Tribulation produces.

God created me to be a father; this I know. It has been a blessing to affirm my sons and daughters. Rest assured, in a manner congruent with how God made me, I sought to perfect, establish, strengthen, and settle my children. I have no higher aim than to affirm my children's worth and potential.

As fathers, we have a profound message to share with our children. May we boldly proclaim:

> God calls you. He calls you through and with struggles. Be sure to listen. In the lightest of afflictions and the darkest of contests, He beckons. Be still and know He is God. Persevere into the character of a victor with a

hope anchored in an unwavering obedience and faith. For, when you are upon the ledge, listen. If at a standstill or ready to capitulate, listen. When you surrender or if you are broken, listen. Amidst the din of battle and confusion of circumstances, He will beckon still.

Listen, dear children. God is by your side. He contends with you upon the ledge. He beckons you with an unfailing love. Listen. He calls you by name. He entreats you. Always on time, God will ask, "What do I always tell you?" May you have the faith to respond, "Trust Daddy!" As you leap from upon the ledge into unknown possibility, your Father, with a knowing nod and outstretched arms, will rejoice with all creation and proclaim, "It is good."

The End

The Ledge

"Jump, Timothy! Jump!" I yelled. "You can do it!" Balanced among the rocks that lined the bottom of a natural pool of water, which ten seconds earlier cascaded over a waterfall ten feet before me, I gazed at my son. My fingers and feet were white, numbed by the frigid water. "Wahoo, Timothy! You are the man!" I shouted over the thunderous pounding. High above, Timothy stood as if frozen in time. He summoned the courage to step off in defiance of his fears.

With his arms wrapped around his chest, Timothy shivered. His knees were bent. His feet were immovable. His eyes were fixed upon the water below. He heard me, but he was not listening. He was trapped within the circumstances before and around him. His mind was plying its trade of deceit and doubt. Timothy's emotions were conflicting. His will balked at the challenge. My precious son, in the throes of life, confronted the possibility of being. Would he jump? How would the experience end? What would he come to understand? The wonder of it all.

Two months prior to Timothy's arrival upon the ledge, he and his sister, Emma, hiked with me over a mile up a mountain that is home to a little-known reservoir which sits on a plateau.

It is a serene setting, picturesque. The water is warm and still, green and clear. At the water's edge, a few flat rocks serve as steps which mark the drop-off into the depths. Minnows and small fish dart about in search of food.

Pronounced above all aspects of this secluded paradise is the quietness. To shout seems unnatural, as if forbidden. Though we had the place to ourselves, our laughter and banter were surreal. Timothy and Emma, who reveled in their curiosity and excitement, were the lone contrast to an otherwise tranquil atmosphere. This was our playground for the day and we made the most of it.

In the left center of the reservoir is a large concrete platform rising twelve feet out of the water. Beginning underneath the surface of the water are rectangular-shaped steel rungs anchored in the side of the structure ascending every eighteen inches to the top. This ladder is the invitation to one of the many battlegrounds in a child's life. The moment my children saw the platform, the only artificial element of the setting, they wanted to jump from the top. So, with floats around their arms, we dived into the small lake and swam some distance to the colossal, tan structure. We climbed the rough rungs to the top and were rewarded with the warmth of sun-baked cement under our tender feet.

Not surprisingly, Timothy's and Emma's perspectives were drastically altered. Their vantage from above the water was strikingly different than the one below. I watched their faces. I sensed their astonishment and trepidation. I noticed their subtle and not so subtle reservations. I wondered if they would change their minds. The endeavor was daring for any young child to ponder, to do what a father would not rightly expect.

Except for the sound of the surplus spilling into the drains at the base of the tower, the water was as calm as it was near the shore. The stillness put Timothy and Emma at ease. We were blanketed in peace. The sky was blue and cloudless. The wind was ever so gentle. There were no rocks visible. If any existed, they were hidden at least thirty feet down.

Would Timothy and Emma jump? They had no pressure to perform and no influence to keep them from doing so. They were with their father, their biggest fan. They knew I would not push them to do what they did not desire. I was there to encourage, regardless of their decision.

Surprisingly, within moments, and to my delight, they did the unexpected. They dropped from the top of the platform and splashed into the expanding depths of who they were to become. I was as proud of them as I was ecstatic.

Now upon the ledge above the waterfall, Timothy faced an experience quite dissimilar from the concrete platform at the reservoir and certainly not as high. He confronted an unexpected challenge of his mind, heart, and will. He would be tested and, whether he prevailed or not, obtain a clearer understanding of himself in the face of adversity. Moreover, even if he did not realize it, in some small measure, he would gain a greater understanding of God and God's will for his life.

As Timothy stood upon the ledge, as I encouraged him, I was struck with the enormity of the scene and pressures upon him. While all struggles are similar in many respects, each has a separate context nonetheless. I am certain God relished the contest of boy against himself as much as I did. This was true the day Emma and Timothy jumped from the platform at the reservoir.

Undoubtedly observers are directly affected by those in the heat of battle. Their observations are defining and add meaning to their lives. Emma was now on the sidelines. Yet, she certainly had an appreciation for Timothy's dilemma. The drop she made at the reservoir was one of the gutsiest and most inspiring. I will never forget how she inched her cute little toes to the edge and then stood motionless. Quite like an Olympic platform diver, she acted only when she knew she was ready. She was as bold as any six-year-old and her form was perfect.

Although Emma made the choice not to jump from the ledge, she vicariously understood her brother's challenge. Additionally, out of love for Timothy, she was vested in his daring effort. She would be influenced not only by the tribulation, but she would be moved by Timothy's performance. The impact may be greater for those on the periphery simply because they generally are unable to affect the outcome. They are beholden to what is.

We traveled to the country to reach this secluded spot. The majestic Shenandoah River is just a stone's throw away. Along a quiet road among the towering sycamores, elms, oaks, and maples, some of which had been there for centuries, a creek catapulted off a ledge and raced to the river. Access to the creek required a steep descent down a thirty-foot trail. To misstep would be to fall. For support, we grabbed vines, branches, and roots lining the path to the water's edge.

The creek was filled with huge rocks and mighty boulders. The noise from the waterfall was deafening. The cliff to the right and dense vegetation to the left trapped the sound. Its only escape was to rise into the moist air or flow with the mist and water downstream. Fifteen feet before us was a pool of water some twelve feet deep. The pool was pounded into submission by the crushing volume of water charging over the ninety-degree drop. The sheer force drove the cool mist directly into our faces. Any remaining water from above flowed discreetly along an embankment to the right that was nearly hidden by low vegetation.

At the center of the ledge was a tree trunk that had fallen and now crossed the creek at a forty-five-degree angle. The trunk rose until it was three feet directly above the ledge. It was as if it had been providentially placed for fathers to make their leaps, which is what I had done.

Directly to the left of the tree trunk, on top of the ledge itself, moss covered rocks were ceremoniously laid for those brave enough to trek across the slippery creek bed. This was the appointed place for those brazen enough to stand in the center of this venue. From this spot, the observer, especially an eight-year-old boy, could be overwhelmed with the confluence of such striking sensations. Vividly accented in the water, rocks and boulders appeared as if they were mere inches from the surface and one could kneel and touch them.

These were the circumstances the day Timothy stood centerstage upon the ledge as he marshaled the gumption to leap. Against this scenic backdrop, fronting this grand but confined and chaotic theater, poised above the imposing below, with the cacophony of bass drums bellowing from the well of the waterfall, as the forest swallowed the creek not fifty feet beyond, Timothy struggled with it all. The atmosphere was loud and violent compared to the tranquillity of the reservoir. There was no doubt my son was now tested in ways he was not upon the concrete platform.

"Timothy!" I yelled over the constant clapping of the waterfall. "This jump is four feet less than the reservoir." Though he acknowledged my observation, he was unaffected. He was transfixed by the torrent and turmoil of his emotions and thoughts. He was affected by any number of factors: the noise, sights, the rocks, mist, the expanse that surrounded the pool, the cliff to the left, and the cold water. Even the peaceful backdrop added to the dramatic tension. To make matters worse, he, unlike the time at the concrete tower, had an audience. Timothy's aunt Holly and cousin Maddie were watching. Pressure powered down upon a boy who wanted to perform.

Timothy wanted to jump. Yet, there is a distinction between wanting and knowing he was not willing. Since I was not inclined to force him against his will, recognizing the harm from such short-sightedness, I did what came naturally. I observed until I knew he needed me to come alongside him and then I would provide encouragement.

I stumbled out of the cold water and reached the base of the trail. I grabbed the roots, vines, and branches and leaned into the ascent. My purpose was clear, as clear as the water that could not hide what lay beneath its surface. I would affirm my son and love him as only a father could. I would share my thoughts and he would express those thoughts into action.

When I reached the path that led to the creek behind the mossy ledge, I darted quickly and negotiated the slippery, flat rocks and walked down the middle of the creek bed until I was at Timothy's side. His hair was still wet, but his skin was dry, save a few beads of water that remained on his narrow shoulders. He continued to crouch, not from the cold, but from permanence of inaction, as if chiseled in stone.

When I looked at him, he dropped his arms. It was then that he broke his silence in a way that would move the stoics and embolden the most fervent of fathers. Lifting his blue eyes to mine, he asked, "Why won't my legs do what my mind tells them?" From the mouths of babes, I was amazed at the poignancy of his question. "Oh my, Timothy," I uttered with admiration, "There are men who live fifty and sixty years who never ask such a profound question."

Though I approach my children as consistently as possible, Timothy's query humbled me. While all events are instructive, a moment such as this was worthy of a father's influence. With ardent passion, but with the skill of a competent coach, I lowered myself to Timothy's eyes. I explained in simple terms what he confronted. I pointed to the obvious, the noise of the waterfall, the cold water, the ominous appearance of the rocks, the confinement of the trees and cliff that enclosed us. I reminded him of his courage at the reservoir and the valiant jump that was four feet higher. I noted his determination, strength, and ability. I explained that his mind was overwhelmed with conflicting thoughts and strong doubts. I shared that his thoughts and emotions were confused which caused him to fear more than to be bold.

I then asked Timothy the only question that mattered. "Do you want to jump?" "Yes," he earnestly replied. I told him he had the will to do so and offered to jump with him. However, I was emphatic. We had to be courageous and choose to act. I explained that, given the slippery rocks, the edge of the ledge was a hazard. We had to be deliberate. We could not doubt. He knew I would not jeopardize his health and well-being with indecision. With a hint of trepidation, Timothy thought for a moment. He then made the choice to jump.

We determined that on the count of three, we would leap. Yet, on three, Timothy was as immovable as he was for the last fifteen minutes. We both looked at each other and started laughing. The comic relief was unexpected, but welcomed. I then encouraged him to reconsider. "No!" he said. He was resolved. This time I clasped his hand. I looked into his eyes and said, "We are going to jump on three." Timothy nodded in agreement. "What do I always tell you, Timothy?" "Trust Daddy," he replied. "One, two, three!"

As I leaped off the ledge, I could not help but notice my arm was fully extended and there was tension between me and Timothy that should not have been. For an instant, I was airborne while he was still held captive to the ledge and his own limitations. I was not going to release my hand. Inevitably, Timothy's frozen frame was freed from that formidable foe waging the brunt of this battle. Two warriors, father and son, were free-falling into the unknown. Two warriors embraced one of the many random variables of possibility manifested in and through struggle.

The inevitable became a reality. Timothy and I descended and plunged into the pool. When we surfaced, I rejoiced in his bravery. "Yahoo!" I exclaimed, as Holly, Maddie, and Emma cheered. "You did it!"

After we swam to shallow waters, I pulled him close and hugged him. "I am so proud of you, Timothy." Surprisingly, not wanting any credit, he looked at me with humility and innocence and said, "I didn't jump, Daddy. You pulled me in." Yet, Timothy did everything he needed to prevail. Little did he know the wealth of understanding he had acquired.

I looked at my son, who was now united with his father in victory, and unquestioningly affirmed that he leapt off the ledge. I underscored that we did it together. He braved tribulation with perseverance which revealed his character and gave him hope. Timothy, to whatever small degree, came to know and understand himself that much more. With yet another tribulation, Timothy came that much closer to knowing himself, God, and His will.

As we made our way to the edge of the creek, I watched my son. He beamed. Yes, something happened that day. Timothy encountered the unknown and, as a result, came to know himself more. God created my son to conquer a ledge and enter a world of possibility. God created me to shepherd my son through dark valleys and Timothy would receive much by persevering through struggle. Such is victory.

When we reached Holly and Maddie, we celebrated. We took satisfaction as witnesses of a boy who battled into victory. Emma admired her brother. Her mind and heart attested to a feat which taught her about his character. Timothy grew immeasurably in her estimation. Whether she realized it or not, Emma was inspired by the manifestation of Timothy being in and battling through tribulation. Emma, Holly, Maddie, and I want, need, and depend upon the resolve of warriors like Timothy, those who dare to venture where many fear to tread.

When we continued our trip to the river, I looked at Timothy. He sat with his hands upon his lap. His countenance reflected both contemplation and joy. His face revealed the hint of a grin which he fought to hide as his eyes glanced to those dear. Timothy could not have adequately expressed what he thought and felt about his victory. He was proud in a humble and satisfying sense. I knew that he knew he had accomplished the unthinkable. I was grateful for my son's growth through a defining tribulation. He was a conquering warrior.

Whether for my son's courageous being from the unknown into understanding, or my choice to affirm a boy as he becomes the man God intends, I took solace in the love I felt. I took quiet satisfaction as I admired the wonder, beauty, and bounty realized in and through tribulation. Timothy and Emma grew that day. This, to me, was the epitome of fatherhood—affirmation of my children. I proclaimed, "It is good." God was glorified. With the sweet aroma of sacrifice—the pinnacle act of worship of a boy who honored both his earthly and heavenly father through tribulation—God was satisfied that it was good. Timothy came to know himself, his God, and God's will by perseverance into character and a hope that will not disappoint.

Acknowledgements

This book was lodged within the recesses of my mind and heart for years. One of the greatest struggles of my life was needed to draw it out. I humbly acknowledge God for the adversity that has tested my soul. I am grateful for the capacity to rightly divide tribulation into greater truth.

With humility, I am grateful to my children. They are and will always be the quintessence of my life. They are the ones who taught me and refined my sensitivities as a man and father. They posed one of the greatest struggles to a life of enlightenment. I am indebted to each.

To the men in prison who endured my oft edited manuscripts, I am thankful for your insight, wisdom, corrections, and candor. Luis, Dave, Rick, Lloyd, Steve, JR, Mac, Chris, John, Griff, Danny, and Orlando, you confirmed and added to a work that would have been less instructive without your input.

To Dave Pruss, the creator of the cover, who captured the ledge in pencil, you have my appreciation.

To those who read The Ledge and were moved to action, this was tremendous insight. The fact that men took notes or wrote letters to their children or recalled their past stands upon the ledges of life was gratifying. The Ledge drew out thoughts and emotions that were latent and in search of expression. For these anecdotal references, which validated Timothy's challenge upon the ledge, I am humbled and deeply appreciative. One man offered the following poem—a testament of his stand upon the ledge as a child.

Leap of Faith

Repairs on our home's roof were done.
The tools back on the ground.
The ladder was on the other side.
I'd have to go around.
I was young and small, it seemed so high.
I felt as tall as a tree.
Beside the tools back down below,
Dad was looking up at me.
"Come on and jump. I'll catch you,"
His arms were open wide.
No doubt his strength's sufficient,
But fear welled up inside.
I looked from Dad back to the ground.
It seemed like such a fall.
Patiently with his strong arms up,
Again, I heard him call.
"You can jump. I'll catch you,"
Again I heard him say.
I'll never forget the sad look in his eyes
As I turned and walked away.
I am reminded of Jesus walking on water
To his disciples out in the boat.
Jesus told Peter to walk to Him,
And stepping out, he stayed afloat!

Peter walked toward Jesus until he looked away.
And then he began to sink.
(Sometimes our greatest troubles start
When we take the time to think.)
I've wondered if there was sadness
In Jesus' eyes that day,
As Jesus stood with outstretched arms
But Peter looked away.
Still, Peter took a leap of faith
In stepping from the boat.
He didn't take the time to think -
"There's no way I should float."
A leap of faith is one small step
Beyond natural human fear.
To step toward the One you trust
And know His strength is near.
Sometimes we fail to consider this
About Peter and our Lord:
After Jesus lifted Peter back up
Peter walked back on board.
Jesus is standing with arms outstretched
And calling you today.
Please turn your eyes upon Jesus,
He's only a leap of faith away.

Lloyd Dean Carder

About the Author

James Bowers Johnson is the father of Cory, Heather, Timothy, and Emma. Born and raised in Virginia, he was graduated from the Virginia Military Institute in 1987. As a Distinguished Military Graduate, he received an Army Commission, served in the field of Military Intelligence, and was Company Commander for HHC, 748th MI Battalion, 704th MI Brigade, INSCOM.

He was unjustly incarcerated for four years for allegedly failing to sign a piece of paper for the federal government. You may read about his incredible story in The End of Justice, a revelation as to why America is the most incarcerated country in the world.

Notes

[1] Genesis 1:31, New International Version

[2] Romans 5:3-5, The Holy Bible, New Kings James Version, Copyright 1982, Thomas Nelson, Inc

[3] Philippians 1:21, New International Version

[4] http://www.theodore-roosevelt.com/trsorbonnespeech.html, "Citizenship In A Republic"

[5] Exodus 3:14, New International Version

[6] Ralph Waldo Emerson, http://www.goodreads.com/quotes/11079-what-you-do-speaks-so-loudly-that-i-cannot-hear

[7] Luke 22:42, New International Version

[8] Philippians 1:21, New International Version

[9] Romans 5:1-2, New International Version

[10] Hebrews 11:1, New International Version

[11] 1 Peter 5:10, New International Version